THE WEIRDEST MOVIE EVER MADE
The Patterson-Gimlin Bigfoot Film

By Phil Hall

THE WEIRDEST MOVIE EVER MADE:
The Patterson-Gimlin Bigfoot Film
Phil Hall
© 2018 Phil Hall. ALL RIGHTS RESERVED.
No part of this book may be reproduced in any form or by any means, electronic, mechanical, digital, photocopying, or recording, except for inclusion of a review, without permission in writing from the publisher or Author.

Published in the USA by:
BearManor Media
P O Box 71426
Albany, Georgia 31708
www.bearmanormedia.com

ISBN: 978-1-62933-356-4
BearManor Media, Albany, Georgia
Printed in the United States of America
Book design by Robbie Adkins, www.adkinsconsult.com

"One day tells its tale to another, and one night imparts knowledge to another.

Although they have no words or language, and their voices are not heard" – Psalm 19:2-3

Table of Contents

Introduction 1

Chapter One: For Your Viewing Pleasure 6

A Bigfoot Interlude: Officer, You Won't Believe This, But… . . 19

Chapter Two: Meanwhile, On the Fringes of Science 20

Bigfoot Interlude: Where the Sasquatch Is (And Is Not) 32

Chapter Three: Bigfoot Steps into Scientific View 33

A Bigfoot Interlude: Why Did the Sasquatch Cross the Road? . . 52

Chapter Four: Bigfoot Cinema 53

A Bigfoot Interlude: Sasquatch vs. E.T. 66

Chapter Five: Bigfoot or Bigfaux? 67

A Bigfoot Interlude: I'm Bigfoot! 75

Chapter Six: Cinematic Appreciation 76

A Bigfoot Interlude: Chanel for Sasquatch? 103

Chapter Seven: The Show is Over 104

Acknowledgements 109

Bibliography 110

About the Author 113

Introduction

"Bigfoot was interviewed on The Patty Winters Show this morning, and to my shock I found him surprisingly articulate and charming."
– Bret Easton Ellis, American Psycho

Back in May 2012, Cornwall, Pennsylvania-based residents Jesse L. Wenrich and Robert E. Zimmerman II were minding their business one night when they heard a very strange noise coming out of a nearby forest. Zimmerman would later explain that the noise sounded "like Jennifer Love Hewitt being stabbed in a horror movie" and, with Wenrich in agreement, he concluded that the source of the noise had to be a Sasquatch.

How did Zimmerman get from a shrieking Point A to a Sasquatch Point B? Well, Jennifer Love Hewitt wasn't shooting horror movies in the area, so she couldn't be blamed. But Zimmerman claimed that he saw a Sasquatch in 1999 on the Appalachian Trail in Pottsville, Pennsylvania, adding that it was "the most beautiful thing I've ever seen in my life." We can assume that he was referring to a spiritual beauty in the hirsute hominid rather than an audio or visual level of charm.

Wenrich and Zimmerman drove off into the night in search of the creature, but they did not get very far: their truck got stuck in the mud on a private residential property development that was punctuated with a surplus amount of "No Trespassing" signs. Rather than making a call on a cell phone for assistance, the men went to a residence on the property and, at 5:05 in the morning, banged on its front door, demanding aid. The property owner, not surprisingly, was terrified by this nonsense and the local police were quickly summoned. The duo was arrested for criminal trespass. The police, it seemed, were not particularly curious to affirm that a Keystone State Sasquatch bearing a vocal resemblance to Jennifer Love Hewitt in an advanced state of disembowelment was in the area, nor did not they bother to have Zimmerman and Wenrich lead them on a search to confirm the men's theory.

Now, let's backpedal a decade to the other end of the gene pool. One of the most respected women in science, the anthropologist and primatologist Dame Jane Goodall, was queried on a September 2002 edition of National Public Radio's program "Science Friday" regarding the genuine nature of the Sasquatch species. Her response generated something of a gasp from the scientific community, which was always very skeptical that Bigfoot was somewhere out there.

"I've talked to so many Native Americans who all describe the same sounds, two who have seen them," she stated. "I've probably got about, oh, 30 books that have come from different parts of the world, from China, from all over the place, and there was a little tiny snippet in the newspaper just last week which says that British scientists have found what they believed to be a yeti hair and that the scientists in the Natural History Museum in London couldn't identify it as any known animal."

When pressed further during the interview as to whether she believed in the existence of the Sasquatch or its Himalayan cousin, the Yeti, Goodall said with a light laugh, "Well, I'm a romantic, so I always wanted them to exist." She then tacked a postscript to her thoughts by noting, "Of course, the big, the big criticism of all this is, 'Where is the body?' You know, why isn't there a body? I can't answer that, and maybe they don't exist, but I want them to."

In October 2012, Goodall was challenged again on the subject, this time by the Huffington Post. One decade after her initial comments, Goodall's opinion remained unchanged.

"I'm not going to flat-out deny its existence," she said. "I'm fascinated and would actually love them to exist. Of course, it's strange that there has never been a single authentic hide or hair of the Bigfoot, but I've read all the accounts."

It is astonishing to consider how the numbskulls in Pennsylvania and the distinguished anthropologist could possibly have anything in common; their shared belief in a mysterious and elusive creature is the unlikeliest of bonds. And this would never have happened had it not been for a weird amateur film depicting an alleged Sasquatch, dubbed Bigfoot, that was shot in a California forest on October 20, 1967. That footage was credited to Roger Patterson and Bob Gimlin – hence, it is known as the Patterson-Gimlin Film.

All of the evidence presented to support the case for Bigfoot's existence – and, in many ways, the most-often cited evidence used to argue that Bigfoot is a myth or a hoax – is rooted in the shaky, grainy color used in the Patterson-Gimlin Film. Not unlike the Zapruder film of the assassination of President John F. Kennedy, the Patterson-Gimlin Film represents the most astonishing of cinematic accidents, where the right people were in the right place at the right time with a movie camera. However, there is a difference between those two films. While no one claims that Zapruder faked the president's assassination, there have been more than a few people who claimed Patterson and Gimlin were trying to pull a hoax.

But were they? In some ways, their footage is the celluloid equivalent of the Rorschach test, that now-clichéd psychological exercise where viewers study a picture of a seemingly enigmatic dark blob and are asked to describe what they see. In this case, the moving image of Bigfoot captured by the Patterson-Gimlin Film is the dark blob, and viewer reaction to it has been varied.

Writer Kyle Hill, in an article published in the October 2013 edition of *Scientific American*, offered a polite dismissal of the notion that Bigfoot was real. "Science – psychology in particular – has shown time and again that human perception is easily distorted, and therefore plain eyewitness testimony in biology or zoology holds little weight," Hill wrote. "In contrast, pseudoscientific endeavors like the continued hunt for Bigfoot use each new eyewitness 'sighting' to increase the likelihood just a little. Innumerable eyewitness reports amount to a 'likely' conclusion in Bigfoot lore because the existence of Bigfoot was decided upon before it was seen."

On the other hand, we have someone like Jeffery Meldrum, a professor of anatomy and anthropology at Idaho State University and one of the few academics to devote serious research to the subject of Sasquatches. When he looks at the film, he knows what he is seeing.

"At this point, I'm as confident as I can be short of standing on the sandbar with Roger and Bob, and witnessing it myself," said Meldrum in a December 2017 interview with Oregon Public Broadcasting. "It's all so easy to say, 'Obviously that's a man in a fur suit.' Until you see it up against a man in a fur suit."

Well, both Hill and Meldrum cannot be right.

But perhaps we are getting a little ahead of ourselves. There would be no debate – and, indeed, this book would not be in front of you – had it not been for the weird images captured by Roger Patterson and Bob Gimlin on their ribbon of film. The story behind the film's creation and release on an unsuspecting world is almost as bizarre as the footage itself.

And how, you may wonder, did all of that come about? Well, as they say in screening rooms, let's roll that footage.

Chapter One
For Your Viewing Pleasure

"You don't make a movie, the movie makes you."
– Jean-Luc Godard

Neither Roger Patterson nor Bob Gimlin had any professional training or experience in film production. A pair of military veterans – Patterson served in the Army, Gimlin in the Navy – their only foray into the entertainment world came briefly as rodeo riders in the 1950s. By the early 1960s, both men had given up on getting tossed from the saddle and sought out placid and inconspicuous lives in the area around Yakima, Washington. Patterson ran a small and none-too-successful fertilizer business while using his spare time to create kitchen gadgets. He devoted a great deal of his leisure time to reading about the Sasquatch, a large and hairy beast that was prevalent in Native American folklore, and by 1966 his obsession with the subject was so pronounced that he wrote and illustrated a book called *Do Abominable Snowmen of America Really Exist?*, which he had published via a small vanity press. Gimlin worked at several jobs, including roofing, truck driving, and horse taming. While he could trace part of his heritage to the Apache Indian nation, he had no interest in the Native American folklore about the Sasquatch.

In August 1967, Patterson learned that strange oversized footprints were found in Northern California's Six Rivers National Forest. He believed that the footprints could be evidence that the Sasquatch stories had some level of reality, and he sought to convince Gimlin that they should travel together to the forest to look for the creature. As Gimlin would later recall, he was initially skeptical but he decided to make the long trip, complete with horses to navigate through the woods, because "I wanted to see these footprints that these people talked about." Patterson was 34 and Gimlin was 35 at the time of their trip, and both left their wives at home to go searching for the Sasquatch.

The footage that became known as the Patterson-Gimlin Film was shot on Friday, October 20, 1967, at the Bluff Creek tributary along the Klamath River in Six Rivers National Forest. This area of the forest was not accessible by automobile, so Patterson and Gimlin parked their vehicle at the forest's entrance and rode into the area on their horses, taking along a third equine as a pack horse. The men carried firearms with them, as the forest was home to bears and cougars.

The entire cinematic output of that day's journey consisted of two reels of Kodachrome II daylight color reversal 16mm film packed into a hand-wound, hand-held Kodak Cine-100 home camera. Each reel ran 100 feet in length, or approximately five minutes. Natural lighting was used to capture all of the images; the camera was silent, and the men did not bring audio recording equipment. In subsequent interviews, Patterson and Gimlin estimated that their footage was shot in the early afternoon, some time between 2:00 p.m. and 4:00 p.m.

The first two-thirds of the initial reel were establishing shots of Patterson riding a horse through the Bluff Canyon wilderness, with a pack horse tethered beside him. Three years earlier, severe storms swept through the area, leaving a surplus of downed trees and dislodged rocks. Gimlin was the cameraman – and for a novice working with a handheld camera, his work was surprisingly steady.

These establishing shots feel more like home movie footage or a test reel. Patterson, bedecked in a wide-brimmed cowboy hat, was shot in an imperfect silhouette atop his horse. In the next shot, Patterson rode away into the distance, with Gimlin keeping his camera almost totally motionless as the horseman receded from view. The scene is relatively brief, but its visual monotony makes it seem endless.

It was obviously a pleasant day, and Gimlin took advantage of the forest's autumnal beauty with slow tracking shots that captured the vast vertical majesty of the trees. Patterson and his horses appeared again, with the camera following them in a leisurely walk through the woods. The pack horse stopped abruptly and seemed to make a snack of some grass. The camera briefly panned away for another peek at the trees and then returned to find Patterson riding directly to the camera. Gimlin panned away into the trees again. Then, there was an abrupt cut as Patterson rode away from the camera again while Gimlin panned into yet another dreamy cinematic meditation on the trees.

These shots took up roughly 75 feet of the 100-foot reel. At some point, Gimlin handed the camera back to Patterson and the two continued on their respective horses.

And then, without warning, all hell broke loose. The footage is wild and blurred and the Bluff Creek ecosystem became a hectic whirl of colors. Patterson later claimed that his horse began to rear, so he was simultaneously attempting to dismount from his agitated animal while keeping the camera operational and focused on something in the distance.

At first, it is difficult to ascertain what Patterson was filming. It appears to be a dark, human-like object walking casually away into the woods. Its posture was slightly off-kilter, with a wide upper body slightly hunched forward while its feet amble in wide, awkwardly rolling steps. It looks to be covered from head to toe in dark fur, but the shadows cast from the woods behind the object make it difficult to observe.

Patterson's camera wobbled violently as he ran after the being, which suddenly began walking away from him at a slightly more deliberate pace. But it did not appear to be threatened by Patterson's presence – it was not running, and its body language (at least through a human measurement) betrayed no evidence of apprehension.

Patterson finally stopped chasing the being on foot and let his camera's zoom lens take over the pursuit. Now we get a better view of the creature that would later be dubbed Bigfoot. It walked across a sandbar and began to retreat from view. But with a steadier camera capturing the scene, we can appreciate its arms, which were swinging in a loose-limbed manner. Oddly, its arms seem a bit too long and willowy for its massive body, which looks like a solid network of overdeveloped muscles blanketed by thin dark fur. Its legs were also unusually thick, but they appear to be in proportion with the body.

With no warning, Bigfoot finally acknowledged the camera. While still walking, its head turned slightly and then its upper torso and face pivoted to look back at Patterson. Its arms swung out to form an inverted V-shape, perhaps to balance this abrupt back-facing twist, and the resulting stretch in its arm-span is astonishing. Bigfoot is too far away for its face to be clearly visible, but later frame enlargements show a simian-type face that is nearly all covered in dark fur. Its unblinking eyes and enigmatic facial expression defied immediate analysis, while its clenched jaws denied us a glimpse into its mouth.

Also visible in this unexpected glance back are long, floppy, fur-covered breasts that dangled from its chest. This is either a female creature or a male with an acute case of gynecomastia.

Bigfoot then turned and moved along at a somewhat quicker pace. Its arms began to swing in a locomotive manner, as if speeding up its exit. It slowly disappeared into the woods and from sight. Patterson's camera shook again as he tried to chase after it on foot, but it is already too late: Bigfoot has exited into the distance and can barely be seen in retreat amid the forest's greatness.

At this point, the first film reel has run its course – Bigfoot took up roughly 25 feet of film, consisting of 954 frames or a shade under 60 seconds.

Patterson reloaded the camera for the second reel, but at that point Bigfoot was nowhere in sight. Instead, Gimlin resumed the duty of cinematographer as Patterson poured plaster into the footprints left behind by Bigfoot. After the plaster cast is made, Patterson is shown standing by a tree while holding the very large footprint casts.

According to film historian William Munns, the second reel also contained Gimlin's only on-camera appearance, in which he leaped off a log and landed on the ground to show the level of impact needed to create the great depth of a footprint left behind by Bigfoot in the Bluff Creek soil. However, that footage is no longer available for review and is believed to have been lost.

What's Wrong with This Picture, Part One

But what is this large and hairy being walking away from the camera? Trying to come up with a quick and simple zoological answer is not easy.

Is it a bear? After all, bears are native to the Bluff Creek region. However, outside of Yogi and Boo-Boo it is uncommon to find bears taking insouciant bipedal strolls through the woods. And, in any event, Bigfoot's physical shape has no resemblance to the ursine anatomy.

At first glance, it would be easy to mistake Bigfoot for a gorilla. Of course, that theory creates more questions – not the least being how an African primate came to assume residency in the California woods. But Bigfoot was moving in an upright (if slightly hunched over) human gait, not in the manner of a gorilla traveling across a landscape by using its extended arms to propel it farther and faster.

So if it is not a real gorilla, could it be a man in a gorilla costume? While skeptics of the footage insist that this being is merely an animal-suited performer, there is a problem with this theory. The gorilla suits of that period were designed to create a broad and burly beast – indeed, they rarely looked like real apes and gave the impression of a burlesque of the jungle primate. Bigfoot on camera is everything that a gorilla-costumed performer from those years was not: extraordinarily tall, with extremely thick legs and muscular shoulders. And few gorilla costumes in the 1960s had long, floppy breasts.

Furthermore, Bigfoot as captured on film bears no resemblance to the wild man concept of the elusive Sasquatch that was depicted in Patterson's hand-drawn illustrations in his book, *Do Abominable Snowmen of America Really Exist?* Patterson's drawings were supposedly based on sightings from earlier in the 20th century, and his book's version was closer in appearance to a caveman. Bigfoot in the film might be walking like a human, but it looks nothing like the commonly held image of a vaguely human caveman. (The cover art for a 1967 reissue of Patterson's book featured a creature that was closer in appearance to a gorilla than a caveman, a reflection of what he captured on film.)

However, the star of the film did have a resemblance to a creature that was allegedly witnessed 12 years earlier at Mica Mountain in British Columbia by William Roe, a construction worker who claimed to have encountered a female Sasquatch while on a hunting trip. Roe, in an affidavit signed two years after his October 1955 sighting, recalled being witness to what he later realized might be the folkloric Sasquatch come to life.

"It was covered from head to foot with dark brown silver-tipped hair," Roe stated. "But as it came closer I saw by its breasts that it was female. And yet, its torso was not curved like a female's. Its broad frame was straight from shoulder to hip. Its arms were much thicker than a man's arms, and longer, reaching almost to its knees. Its feet were broader proportionately than a man's, about five inches wide at the front and tapering to much thinner heels. When it walked it placed the heel of its foot down first, and I could see the grey-brown skin or hide on the soles of its feet … The head was higher at the back than at the front. The nose was broad and flat. The lips and chin protruded farther than its nose. But the hair that covered it, leaving bare only the parts of its face around the mouth, nose, and ears, made it resemble an animal as much as a human. None of this hair, even on the back of its head, was longer than an inch, and that on its face was much shorter. Its ears were shaped like a human's ears. But its eyes were small and black like a bear's. And its neck also was unhuman. Thicker and shorter than any man's I had ever seen."

Roe's credibility was never publicly called into question, if only because his sighting was ignored by everyone except the fringe cryptozoology media of the era and the devotees of the subject, including Patterson. If, as critics of the Patterson-Gimlin Film insist, the Sasquatch was a costumed performer, then it seems obvious the costume in question was modeled after the Sasquatch described by Roe.

Patterson would later theorize that the Sasquatch encountered at Bluff Creek was elderly and either blind or near-blind, owing to its reaction to the men and its presence in broad daylight. The creatures of tribal folklore were mostly nocturnal, he added, and some tales suggested violent behavior when provoked. But whether the Sasquatch was old, young, or middle-aged is impossible to tell. And the subject of the film could clearly see the men, while having no problems navigating a landscape littered with fallen trees and rocks, which seems to rule out the notion that it was afflicted with any significant visual impairment.

There are elements of the encounter between Patterson and Gimlin and the mysterious creature that are absent from the film. The first involves just how they connected: the men became aware of Bigfoot's presence by its scent, which they described as a debilitating aroma that polluted the clear forest air. But the men did not initially see Bigfoot. Instead, their horses became alarmed by its presence, even though it was at least 100 feet away from them, and the equine agitation cued Patterson and Gimlin to take a closer look.

Also absent from the footage was the Sasquatch's initial response to seeing them. According to Gimlin, Patterson first saw Bigfoot slightly crouched by the creek, where it may have been refreshing itself with water. When Gimlin saw it, Bigfoot was standing and watching them as they approached on horseback, making no effort to approach or retreat upon initial contact, nor did it make any sound. It only began to walk away after Patterson dismounted from his frightened horse and chased after it with his movie camera.

What's Wrong with This Picture, Part Two

And that, in the proverbial nutshell, is the brief but convoluted story of how Bigfoot became the star of the Patterson-Gimlin Film. But from a production standpoint, there are several hiccups in this story.

First, why was there only one movie camera on this expedition? To offer a bowdlerized riff on a beloved observation, excrement happens – and the likelihood of a camera being damaged or malfunctioning, especially when cameramen were riding about on horseback in the woods, was more than possible. Granted, Patterson and Gimlin were working on the barest of budgets and with the scantest of cinematic know-how, so they could not bring a wealth of equipment or Filmmaking 101 planning to the forest. But if they were trying to document the Sasquatch on film, they were incredibly confident in their abilities to outrun Murphy's Law.

The problem with the single camera is obvious from the surplus amount of footage involving trees and Patterson on horseback versus the minimal amount of footage with Bigfoot. A back-up camera could have given us a further examination of the furry forest denizen from another angle.

Second, why wasn't there a still camera ready for photographic evidence? Gimlin reportedly reached for a firearm while Patterson was filming, but he opted not to shoot his gun. But if he had a still camera, there could have been additional coverage of the event taking place.

Third, why did Patterson and Gimlin only leave a minute's worth of film in their camera? If they had an appropriate number of film reels, their first reel could have been set aside exclusively for the establishing shots of Patterson's horseback riding and the seemingly endless panning shots of the trees, while a fresh and full second reel would available for Bigfoot.

But, in some ways, the notion of a Sasquatch schlepping across a sandbar is the least problematic aspect of the Patterson-Gimlin Film's history. When queried afterwards, Patterson and Gimlin and other parties who became involved in their adventure offered information that did not quite compute.

For starters, there was the question of where the film was processed. Patterson and Gimlin initially claimed that they sent the film via airmail to Patterson's brother-in-law, Al DeAtley, in Yakima. DeAtley received it on October 21 – a Saturday, the day after the film was shot – and he had it processed that day for viewing with Patterson and Gimlin when they returned home from Bluff Creek on Sunday, October 22.

However, this creates new problems. You will recall that the Bigfoot encounter took place in the early afternoon. Gimlin would later state in an interview that plaster was used to preserve the Sasquatch footprints. But the plaster was not among their supplies during the encounter. Instead, it was stored in their automobile at their base camp on the outskirts of the forest. This required a three-and-a-half-mile ride back to the base camp to pick up the plaster and a return trip of equal time to make the molds. By the time the molds were completed and the pair left the forest to go to the nearest city, Eureka, the post office would have been closed when Patterson and Gimlin showed up.

Did Patterson and Gimlin hire a charter flight to fly the footage to DeAtley out of the area's small airport? No record of such a flight exists – and, considering the men were very limited in their finances, it is unlikely that they could have produced the cash to plunk down for a very expensive last-second charter flight. And, quite frankly, why would they have trusted the film to a carrier when they could have driven the footage home, which was only a day's drive away?

There is also the problem that neither Patterson, Gimlin, nor DeAtley could recall where the film was processed. Assuming that DeAtley received the reel during the morning or early afternoon of October 21, he would still need to find a film processing lab that was open on a Saturday and was willing to do a rush job. There is no record of any film processing lab in the surrounding vicinity of Yakima that handled this project, which also would have required funds that the men probably did not have.

However, Christopher L. Murphy, author of *Bigfoot Film Journal*, theorized that the film was processed in a non-commercial private home lab and not at a professional facility. Murphy noted the observation of a professional photographer who theorized that the Patterson-Gimlin Film was overexposed when it was processed, hence its washed-out color palette. But Patterson would vaguely yet ominously insist during an interview with the Victoria, British Columbia, *Times Colonist* that the processing was not "done at a private place – it would jeopardize the man's job if it were told." Does this mean that someone sneaked in after hours to process the film, or does that affirm Murphy's notion that the film was ineptly processed at someone's home? The answer to that mystery has yet to surface.

Furthermore, Patterson expressed confusion as to whether he shot the film at a 16 frames per second speed or at an 18 or 24 frames per second speed. This makes a big difference when trying to measure the pacing that the Sasquatch showed in its trek across the screen.

More peculiar is the inconsistency on how long Patterson and Gimlin were at Bluff Creek. Gimlin would claim that the men arrived at the California location on October 1, 1967, which would have put them at the location for three weeks. Yet in an interview published by the *Humboldt Times-Standard* on the day after the encounter, Patterson said that they arrived on October 14. Again, the lack of consistency on simple facts is disturbing. And why did they only decide to play with their movie camera on the day they encountered Bigfoot?

There is also a somewhat more troubling problem regarding this endeavor. As you will recall, Patterson piqued Gimlin's interest in August 1967 about the reports of oversized footprints at Bluff Creek. One could easily assume that Patterson obtained his 16mm camera prior to their departure from Yakima to California.

Instead, Patterson rented the camera from Shepard's Camera Shop in Yakima on May 13, 1967, for what was intended to be a two-day lease. On October 17, a warrant was issued by the Superior Court of Yakima County ordering Patterson's arrest for grand larceny. Patterson evaded apprehension because he spent much of the next few weeks after the Bluff Creek encounter on the road promoting the Bigfoot film, and the warrant was not served until November 28. After being arrested, Patterson pleaded not guilty and was released upon his own recognizance. The case against him was dismissed on December 8, 1969.

Patterson never spoke to reporters about his problems with the camera's ownership, so it is unknown why he opted to take the camera five months before the trip to California – not to mention why he failed to return it to the store upon returning home. Gimlin could not be blamed for the chicanery; he would later state that he was under the belief that Patterson owned the camera.

Furthermore, writer Greg Long uncovered evidence that Patterson made efforts in 1966 to secure a copyright on the word "Bigfoot," but was unsuccessful. Was Patterson so wildly confident that he would secure moving picture imagery of a Sasquatch that he wanted to ensure that he held the rights to the "Bigfoot" name ahead of capturing these images?

If you're already a bit baffled by the shenanigans surrounding this brief bit of film, now is a good time to pause for a refreshment or a breath of fresh air – which will be helpful, because the story gets even more convoluted.

A Bigfoot Interlude: Officer, You Won't Believe This, But…

On March 25, 2017, the Associated Press reported that a driver in northern Idaho blamed a Sasquatch for her collision with a deer.

The 50-year-old woman, who was not publicly identified, said she was driving south on U.S. Highway 95 when she struck a deer near the town of Potlatch. The woman told the Benewah County Sheriff's Department that, while she was driving, she witnessed a Sasquatch chasing a deer along the side of the road. As she attempted to get a better view of the Sasquatch, the deer ran bolted away from its furry predator and ran fatally into the front of her car. The Sasquatch, realizing that venison was off the menu, reportedly disappeared from the scene, leaving the woman with a dented car and a dead deer.

The sheriff's officials filed a report as an incident involving a vehicular collision with a deer. However, the sheriff omitted all mention of the Sasquatch from the final report.

Chapter Two
Meanwhile, On the Fringes of Science...

"Mystery creates wonder, and wonder is the basis of man's desire to understand" – Neil Armstrong

Bigfoot was never embraced by the established scientific disciplines of anthropology and zoology. However, it has been a prominent resident in the realm of cryptozoology ever since it turned up in the Patterson-Gimlin Film.

The term "cryptozoology" – the study of animals whose existence or survival is disputed or unsubstantiated – was coined in the late 1940s by Ivan T. Sanderson, a Scottish-born American biologist whose career veered from botany and ethnography into a funkier pursuit of phenomena that were mostly ignored by mainstream science. The concept of cryptozoology began to take root in modern times thanks to Bernard Heuvelmans, a French scientist and explorer whose 1958 book, *On the Track of Unknown Animals,* offered a global consideration of the topic.

But cryptozoology preceded Sanderson and Heuvelmans, going back to the beginning of civilization. Indeed, the belief in remarkable creatures of bizarre appearance and marvelous physical powers has been a hallmark of nearly every cultural heritage throughout human history. In many societies, the existence of these beings is widely accepted as fact, even though physical evidence is scant, at best.

Consider the Bible, where the massive sea monster called the Leviathan is referenced in Job, Amos, Psalms and Isaiah. Job also mentions the Behemoth, a powerful land creature, and the apocryphal Book of Enoch has Leviathan, Behemoth, and their airborne ally Ziz in a grand collection of extraordinary monsters. (Ziz also flew in early translations of Psalm 50:11 and Psalm 80:13-14, but modern theologians erased that specific reference in favor of a more generic mention of animals.)

Elsewhere in early versions of the Bible, we find Daniel slaying a Babylonian dragon – not with a sword, but by overfeeding it with cakes made from pitch, hair, and fat. The gluttonous creature clearly had poor taste in pastries and no sense of self-control, for it ate Daniel's cooking until it fatally burst. However, that tale turned out to be a little too much for both Jewish and Protestant theologians, who excised it from their respective versions of the sacred texts and dumped it in a collection of jettisoned Bible chapters known as the Apocrypha.

And how can we forget that Jonah was swallowed and imprisoned for three days within the belly of an unidentified marine creature which eventually spat him out on dry land? The Bible only refers to it as a fish, but there is no known species of fish that can consume an adult human. Nor is there any known species of whale that can impose the punishment that Jonah received. Jonah's adventure is also repeated in the Qu'ran, which informs us: "Had it not been that he (repented and) glorified Allah, He would certainly have remained inside the Fish till the Day of Resurrection."

Within the world of cryptozoology, there is an astonishing array of creatures roaming about throughout the world, often occupying the folklores of peoples who could not have cross-pollinated their tales with distant lands. For example, dragons have turned up across the diverse traditions of Europe, Asia, and Africa. Nor is this the exclusive realm of pagan storytelling –

most Christians today know of St. George for his dragon-slaying heroism rather than his piety.

And there are more cryptozoological wonders to be found in the water. Tales of massive lake inhabitants span the world: Scotland's celebrated Loch Ness Monster (a.k.a. Nessie); Japan's Issie and Kussie; Canada's Ogopogo, Manipogo, Igopogo, Memphre, Turtle Lake Monster and Hapyxelor (a.k.a. Mussie); Italy's Lauriosauro, Congo's Mokele-mbembe, Norway's Selma, Laos' Phaya Naga, Iceland's Lagarfljótsormur, Turkey's Lake Van Monster, Argentina's Nahuelito, Ireland's Muckie; South Africa's Inkanyamba and Mamlambo, Russia's Brosnya, and the United States' Altie, Bessie, Champ, Chessie, Sharlie and Tahoe Tessie. It is somewhat astonishing to consider that these diverse cultures, which existed for centuries with no direct contact between each other, would all share that level of cryptozoological tale-spinning.

Furthermore, there is a line-up of cryptid birds, cats, canines, deep sea creatures, and humanoid beings that could fill an entire book – but not this book. You get the idea.

Lights, Camera, Creature

The advent of photography should have been the clincher to bring some of these creatures out of scientific exile in cryptozoology and into the realm of accepted scientific fact. After all, how can one argue with photographic evidence?

Very easily, it turned out, because faking photographic evidence is nearly as old as the technology itself. And photographs often tend to generate more inquisitive questions rather than establishing be-all/end-all answers.

A big breakthrough in proving the existence of fantastic creatures was the so-called "surgeon's photograph" of the Loch Ness Monster that was published in Britain's *Daily Mail* in 1934.

The slightly blurry black-and-white photograph was credited to a medical professional who did not want to be publicly identified, and the image of the creature lifting its serpentine neck from the lake was long considered to be the much-desired evidence that Nessie was real.

Except that it wasn't. In December 1975, Britain's *Sunday Telegraph* published the first article that called out the photograph as a hoax. In 1999, David Martin and Alastair Boyd's book *Nessie – the Surgeon's Photograph Exposed* provided extraordinary depth on the individuals behind the fraud, revealing the detailed plan that was necessary to create the faux-Nessie and frame the prop in Loch Ness in a manner that would create the perfect photograph.

But if still imagery can be disproved, what about moving pictures? The post-World War II mania for unidentified flying objects – then referred to as "flying saucers" – was routinely dismissed in the mainstream media because of the lack of proof that something (or someone) was zooming about in the skies. Despite a history of still photographs of unexplained aircraft dating back to 1870, the skeptics were still unconvinced that uninvited visitors were up in the clouds.

That changed in August 1950 when Nick Mariana, the general manager of the Great Falls Electrics, a minor-league baseball team in Great Falls, Montana, shot 16 seconds of color 16mm film that featured a pair of silvery-white objects moving in perfect unison on a horizontal route across the sky. Reports of Mariana's film filtered into the news, but the general public only got to see it when it was included in the 1956 docu-drama *Unidentified Flying Objects*. Complicating matters was Mariana's claim that the U.S. Air Force removed 35 frames from his film. That part of the film, according to Mariana in a later interview, "showed larger images of the UFOs with a notch or band at one point by which they could be seen to rotate in unison." The Air Force vigorously denied that any footage was removed, but it didn't matter – the notion of a massive government conspiracy to suppress knowledge of extra-terrestrial visitors was permanently enforced.

Now, the Mariana film did not effectively prove that E.T. and his pals took a left turn at Alpha Centauri and went for a joyride over the Montana landscape. But it gave a new infusion of seriousness into a conversation that many people were eager to dismiss over a lack of physical evidence. And for those who were eager to dismiss the so-called "flying saucers" as silliness, the motion picture footage proved that something was up there which defied breezy explanations.

Enter Bigfoot

During the 19th century, European explorers and scholars making their way through the Himalayas were introduced to the notion of the Yeti, a furry bipedal being that supposedly lived in the mountains. Depending on who was telling the story, the creature was either uncommonly timid and would run from the sight of people, or its presence would be a harbinger of death for any poor soul that made eye contact with it. The creature took on a new importance when the 1921 Mount Everest Reconnaissance Expedition came across mysterious footprints at a high altitude where no human community was ever known to exist. While the British leaders of the expedition attributed the footprints to a wolf, the Sherpa guides insisted they belonged to the "metch kangmi" – roughly translated from Nepalese as "filthy snowman." Newspaper reporter Henry Newman cleaned up the "filthy snowman" into a new translation as "abominable snowman" – and for decades after, the Yeti was more commonly known in the West as the Abominable Snowman.

But the Himalayan cultures were not alone in having a mysterious furry hominid as a resident. The Chinese insist that a Yeren roams its mountains, while Vietnam is home to the Batatut, Afghanistan has the Barmanou, India and Bangladesh have their Mande Burung. The Philippines has the Amomongo, Japan has the Hibagong, Indonesia has the Orang Pendek, Malaysia has the Orang Mawas, and Siberia has the Chuchunya.

None of these Asian fur-covered hominids has ever been captured, either dead or alive, nor has any fossil or fur sample been brought forward. As luck would have it, Asia was home to a great ape-like creature whose presence has been scientifically confirmed: the Gigantopithecus stood nearly 10 feet tall and resided across a stretch of territory occupied by today's China, India, and Vietnam. Its extinction is placed at approximately 100,000 years ago. But is it possible that some specimens might have existed longer? There is precedent for supposedly extinct creatures of prehistoric eras turning up long after they were supposed to have vanished: the rediscovery of the coelacanth in 1938 was one of the most important events in marine biology, while unverified sightings of the moa, New Zealand's massive flightless bird, continued well into the 19th century. And while there is no evidence that any of Asia's furry hominids descended from Gigantopithecus, there is the slightest of chances that this creature somehow survived long enough for early humans to witness and record its existence.

But in the North American West Coast, the tradition of furry hominids in the woods becomes a bit more perplexing. Wishful thinking that Bigfoot is a descendant of Gigantopithecus seems unreasonable, as no fossil of this Asian creature was ever located across the Pacific.

Nonetheless, the constellation of tribal nations of North America populated their respective folklores with tales of large, hairy wild creatures that lived in the woods. The personalities attributed to these creatures depends on which native tribe was spinning the story. Some of these beings were allegedly evil, and the tribal legends warned of avoiding contact at all costs. Other beings were supposedly afraid of humans and would only dare venture out at night when people were sleeping. All of these tales were passed down via oral histories; the tribes had no concept of publishing, so there are no drawings to illustrate what the creatures may have looked like.

Each tribe had a different name for its elusive creature, but there were similarities among their designations. For example, in the Pacific Northwest the Clallam-language peoples referred to the "Seeahtkch," while the Salishan-language peoples had the "Saskets" and the Kwakiutl-language speakers had the "Tsonaqua."

The origin of "Sasquatch" is debated, with some sources claiming it was very roughly translated from native languages bye white settlers in what later became British Columbia, while others give the honor to J.W. Burns, a teacher on the Chehalis Indian Reserve near the Harrison River, about 60 miles east of Vancouver. Burns compiled the region's native folklore and published an article in *MacLean's* magazine in 1927 that defined the creature based on the Halkomelem-language "Sasahevas." Burns compiled several supposed eyewitness accounts of encounters with these unclassified beings, concluding that their existence should not be dismissed as silly Indian mythology.

"Is it possible that primitive hairy giants still inhabit the mountain solitudes of British Columbia?" he wrote. "Scientists and others may scoff at the very idea, but many Indians are sincerely convinced that Sasquatch – or at least a few of them -- live to this day in the vast, unexplored interior. And like my Indians, I also believe."

But tribal folklore involving hair-covered wild men is not unique to the Pacific Northwest. Indian nations as far afield as the Seneca of the Northeast, the Hopi, Taos and Zuni of the Southwest, and the Yu'pik and Alutiq of Alaska have legends of giant, human-like creatures haunting their lands.

The oldest recorded sighting of an ape-like creature in North America by a white man is attributed to Leif Ericson in 986 AD. In his first New World landing on today's Newfoundland, the Norse explorer wrote about oversized men who were "horribly ugly, hairy, swarthy and with great black eyes." These beings lived in the woods and had an odor that left an unpleasant after-effect. Ericson dubbed the creature "Skellring," the Norse word for "barbarian."

(Oddly enough, the white men who would usurp the Indians' historical homelands traced their lineage to European countries where similar legends of wild hairy men living in the woods permeated the heritage of the Old World. However, none of these men were mistaken for a simian-type creature.)

Rev. Elkanah Walker, a missionary in Washington State who brought Christianity to the Spokane Indians, wrote in his 1840 diary about a "race of giants, which inhabit a certain mountain off to the west of us" that left great footprints on the ground. Rev. Walker said the Indians spoke of these foul-smelling creatures stealing food from fishing nets and even kidnapping sleeping people.

In 1884, the *Daily Colonist* newspaper in British Columbia published an article about a gorilla-type creature that was reportedly captured in the woods. Bigfoot researchers have wondered if this was creature, which was dubbed Jacko by its captors, was a Sasquatch. Other researchers wonder if the creature ever existed at all – and a surplus amount of evidence supports the notion that Jacko was a hoax story.

One of the first recorded encounters between white men and the simian-type creatures was written by Theodore Roosevelt, of all people. In his 1892 book *The Wilderness Hunter*, Roosevelt told the story of a North American trapper named Bauman whose campsite was reportedly trashed by an unknown animal – and the footprint evidence suggested the animal was bipedal. Bauman's trapping partner was later killed by an animal that broke his neck, and Bauman fled the campsite in fear. However, Bauman never saw the creature that supposedly killed his partner, and Roosevelt offered no commentary on what the creature might have been.

Elsewhere in The *Wilderness Hunter*, Roosevelt recalled a hunting trip in Washington State where he heard very strange noises outside his campsite in an area that his Indian guide recommended avoiding. Roosevelt never theorized what the source of the noises were, but he certainly found them unpleasant.

Another early published report on unusual encounters with unidentified creatures in the Northwest involved an alleged attack on a miners' cabin in 1924 at the southeast shoulder of Mount St. Helens in the state of Washington. The miners claimed that a group of ape-like creatures hurled rocks at their shelter and tried to break in during a twilight rampage. News of the occurrence was published in the July 16, 1924 issue of *The Oregonian*, but no physical evidence of the alleged non-human marauders was ever located.

Also in 1924, a Canadian prospector named Albert Ostman claimed to have been kidnapped and held captive for six days by four Sasquatches in the woods near Toba Inlet in British Columbia. However, Ostman did not publicly tell his story until 1957, and there were many who greeted his tale with skepticism. Yet Ostman never wavered in his account of what supposedly occurred, and he even confronted a hostile critic by stating, "I don't care a damn what you think."

The name "Bigfoot" was coined in connection with the Sasquatch on October 5, 1958. On that date, Andrew Genzoli, a writer at *The Humoldt Times* in the California North Coast city of Eureka, authored a page one story about the discovery of fantastically large humanoid footprints by a road crew working near Bluff Creek along the Klamath River.

"There is a mystery in the mountains of northeastern Humboldt County, waiting for a solution," Genzoli wrote. "Who is making the huge 16-inch tracks in the vicinity of Bluff Creek? Are the tracks a human hoax? Or, are they actual marks of a huge but harmless wild-man, traveling through the wilderness? Can this be some legendary sized animal?"

Genzoli added that the workers at the construction site coined a nickname for the person or thing that was supposedly the source of the footprint: Big Foot. His article also featured a photo of Jerry Crew, a member of the construction team, solemnly holding a plaster cast of one of the footprints.

The story would not go away. *The Humboldt Standard*, a sister publication of the *Times*, published a story that a $1,000 reward was being offered for anyone who would step forward and explain the origins of the footprints. The newspaper wondered if the footprints were the result of a hoax or if they belonged to "a mentally deficient, over-grown boy gone wild."

Ten days later, *Times'* reporter Bill Chambers filed a news story that the Humboldt County Sheriff's Office believed they knew who was behind the footprints. Their suspicion focused on Ray Wallace, a construction worker at the Bluff Creek site. But when Chambers contacted Wallace, the latter was insistent on his innocence.

"I'm not going in," Wallace stated. "If they want to put out a warrant I'm going to sue them for slander – and I won't fool around about it. If they think they're going to make a laughing stock out of me, they've got another think coming."

On October 15, 1958, Chambers wrote another article claiming that "Bigfoot had been seen" by two construction workers. The *Standard* ran its own story the next day, adding that the witnesses were "two husky construction workers with good eyesight."

At that point, the newspapers abruptly lost interest in finding the source of the oversized footprints and moved on to other matters. Ray Wallace died in 2002, and after his passing his son and nephew contacted the *Seattle Times* to confirm that Wallace was the creator of the Bluff Creek footprints. Even more remarkable, June Beal, the widow of *Times'* editor L.W. Beal, stepped forward to admit that her late husband was aware that the story was phony.

"They were in on this hoax," Beal said about the hitherto-unknown scheme between her husband and Wallace. "It was just a fun thing and the fun got out of hand."

Indeed, it got way out of hand. In 1959, a Texas millionaire named Tom Slick financed an expedition to locate the elusive

Bigfoot around Bluff Creek. An Irish big-game hunter named Peter Byrne was imported to lead the expedition; Byrne and Slick made similar journeys in Asia in search of the Abominable Snowman. All of their odysseys, however, turned up nothing.

Nonetheless, curiosity over the presence of Bigfoot around Bluff Creek did not abate. One person in particular seemed to have an insatiable appetite concerning all things related to Bigfoot: Roger Patterson. In the summer of 1967, new Bigfoot tracks were reportedly found at Bluff Creek, which piqued Patterson's interest.

And from here, we now rejoin the story of the Patterson-Gimlin Film.

A Bigfoot Interlude: Where the Sasquatch Is (And Is Not)

When it comes to Sasquatch sightings, the West Coast has the greatest number of people who claim to have run into the elusive hominid.

The Bigfoot Field Research Organization (BFRO) compiled a database that, as of January 2018, included 642 reported sightings in Washington, 437 in California and 245 in Oregon. Other states with multiple reports of Sasquatch activity include Florida (312 sightings), Illinois (287), Ohio (273), and Texas (229).

Most American states are blessed with a Bigfoot. Hawaii is the only state where there has never been a Sasquatch sighting. Other states with a minimal Bigfoot presence include Rhode Island and Delaware (5 sightings each), North Dakota (6 sightings), Nevada (8 sightings), Vermont (9 sightings), and Connecticut (12 sightings).

Chapter Three
Bigfoot Steps into Scientific View

"Cinema is a matter of what's in the frame and what's out." – Martin Scorsese

The first public acknowledgement of the Patterson-Gimlin Film occurred on October 21, 1967, the day after the Bluff Creek encounter. On that Saturday morning, readers of the *Humboldt Times-Standard* – the successor to the newspaper that coined the name "Bigfoot" in 1958 – greeted its readers with a page-one exclusive carrying the headline "Mrs. Bigfoot Is Filmed!"

And how did the newspaper get that scoop? After leaving the forest where the encounter took place, Patterson and Gimlin drove to the town of Willow Creek, where Patterson's friend Al Hodgson owned a store. The store was closed by the time they arrived, so Patterson contacted Hodgson from a pay phone, who returned to the store and opened it for the men.

With Hodgson's consent, Patterson made two long-distance calls: one to his brother-in-law Al DeAtley, informing him of what transpired and telling him to expect the delivery of the films from Bluff Creek. He then called Don Abbott, an anthropologist in British Columbia who was familiar with Bluff Creek from the previous reports of oversized footprints in the area. Patterson reportedly asked Abbott to bring hunting dogs down to Bluff Creek to search for the Sasquatch.

The next telephone call was – mercifully, for the sake of Hodgson's phone bill – a local contact to the *Times-Standard*.

The newspaper's coverage did not carry a byline, but Sasquatch researcher Christopher L. Murphy identified the possible author as Al Tostado, a reporter for the newspaper. We do not know if Patterson's inquiry was a cold call or if he had been in contact with the reporter prior to going into the forest. In any event, the reporter seemed to be familiar with the folklore surrounding the Sasquatch and the XXL-sized footprints that kept turning up in the area.

In retrospect, it seems curious that the newspaper would run the story, let alone put in on its front page. For starters, Patterson and Gimlin had no still photographs or other physical evidence to back the claim of a Sasquatch encounter.

The article also planted many of the seeds of confusion that would baffle and bother scholars trying to make sense of this story. This is obvious from the over-excited first paragraph: "A Yakima, Wash., man and his Indian tracking aide came out of the wilds of northern Humboldt County yesterday to breathlessly report that they had seen and taken motion pictures of 'a giant hominoid creature.'"

This article established the story that Patterson was the brains, heart, and soul of the expedition, with Gimlin relegated to sidekick status. As per the journalistic protocol of that distant era, Gimlin is defined by his race.

The article spends two paragraphs describing Patterson's authorship of the book *Do Abominable Snowmen of America Really Exist?* along with his "50 tapes of interviews" with people who claimed to have seen Sasquatches and the "eight years on the project" that he devoted to the search. Gimlin's knowledge of the subject is ignored, and he is only mentioned as having "been associated with Patterson for a year."

Furthermore, the article stated that Patterson claimed Gimlin released their horses in the commotion of the encounter, although Gimlin would later contradict that. Patterson also affirmed the Sasquatch's gender by saying, "I could see its breasts hanging down and they flopped when it moved" – but Gimlin would later insist they were unaware of the breasts until they reviewed the film footage.

Patterson told the reporter that the film was "already on its way by plane to his hometown for processing," but, as stated earlier, there is no record of a chartered flight flying the film to Yakima and no clear evidence that Patterson had funds with him to pay for a last-minute charter flight. Patterson also identified Al DeAtley as a "partner" who "helped finance Patterson's expeditions," ignoring the fact that DeAtley was his brother-in-law.

The article also quoted Patterson as claiming the Sasquatch encounter happened at 1:30 p.m., adding that it was eight hours prior to the interview with the reporter. However, there has been uncertainty regarding just when the Sasquatch was seen. Assuming the reporter was called at 9:30 p.m., the turnaround time for writing and editing the article and setting it as a page one story would have been uncommonly rapid, especially for a Saturday edition of a small daily newspaper.

The only drop of doubt injected into the interview was the reporter's comment on the varying sizes of so-called Bigfoot footprints found in the area. "The writer jested that that these sizes put him in mind of the Three Bears," he wrote. Patterson humorlessly responded, "We have seen some bears on this trip. This definitely was no bear."

The article concluded that Patterson expressed his need to "telephone his experience to a museum administrator who is also extremely interested in the project." We have no clue as to who this administrator might have been.

Gimlin was never quoted in the article; whether Patterson intentionally kept him off the phone call or whether the reporter chose not to speak with the "Indian tracking aide" is not known. As a result, Patterson was the center of the attention in the first media mention of the footage.

Gimlin drove the pair back to Yakima – he would later claim that Patterson was a terrible driver and he did not trust him to get them home in one piece. Just when they returned, either on late Saturday, October 21 or early Sunday, October 22, is not known. But Gimlin, reported to be exhausted from the drive, went straight to his house to collapse into a lengthy sleep.

The Sasquatch on the Screen

On October 22, Al DeAtley arrived at Patterson's home with the film from Bluff Creek. They were joined by Canadians John Green and René Dahinden, respectively a newspaper publisher and a Swiss-born government forestry officer, who shared an enthusiasm for Sasquatch research, along with a Californian Sasquatch researcher named Jim McClarin. In Patterson's basement, the men viewed the Bigfoot footage and held a lengthy discussion on how to proceed with the film.

Green and Dahinden convinced Patterson that the film should be taken for review before anthropologists at the University of British Columbia in Vancouver. Their argument was solid: The Sasquatch was a more familiar aspect of the British Columbian folklore, and the possibility of documentary evidence would be treated with a greater degree of respect than if the footage was taken to an East Coast university where the Sasquatch was an unknown entity. Joining this cause was Donald Abbott, an archeologist with the Royal British Columbia Museum, who was able to arrange for his institution to study the film.

Starting on October 23, Abbott helped to stir publicity for the film by alerting the media in British Columbia about the existence of the film. A Vancouver radio show host named Jack Webster agreed to interview Patterson and Gimlin when they arrived in the city. During this interview, Webster was the first person to publicly question why Patterson shot the Sasquatch with his camera and not with a gun. "I don't think you would have if you had seen the humanness of it," Patterson responded. "I think it would take a person with a little bit of murder in his heart to shoot something like this."

On October 26, a screening was arranged at the University of British Columbia. For all of the hoopla that was generated about the presentation, the audience turnout was rather scant. Historian Christopher L. Murphy noted there were only two university professors, three museum scientists including Abbott, along with Patterson, Gimlin, Green, Dahinden and another Sasquatch researcher named Bob Titmus. Patterson provided the plaster casts of the footprints collected from the Bluff Creek site for review.

The screening, to be charitable, was a disaster. Frank Beebe, a museum scientist, would recall the presentation in a December 1967 interview by dismissing the creature in the film as "a phony and a fake." Ian McTaggart-Cowan, one of the university scientists who was also present, looked back at the screening in a 1983 interview by stating no one present "thought they were looking at a species of creature unknown to modern science."

Green and Dahinden were hopeful that the presentation in Vancouver would lead to financial backing from the provincial British Columbia government for further Sasquatch research.

Despite an eloquent plea from Abbott supporting that endeavor, the provincial government did not open its wallet for Sasquatch studies.

Returning home from Vancouver, Patterson loaned a copy of the footage to the news department at KIMA, the television station serving the Yakima market. The station broadcast a news item on the alleged encounter and offered a glimpse of the Bluff Creek Sasquatch footage. This represented the first telecast of the Patterson-Gimlin film.

The *Yakima Herald*, the local daily newspaper, ran a brief item on the Bluff Creek Sasquatch with an October 27, 1967, dateline. The article mentioned "25 feet of motion picture film" but offered no imagery. However, a photo of Patterson and Gimlin admiring the plaster casts of the Sasquatch's footprints ran with the story, which was picked up by the Associated Press news wire. It is not certain how many newspapers reran the story via the Associated Press, but this would have been the first wide scale U.S. media acknowledgment of what transpired.

Perhaps smarting from the response in Vancouver that their film was a hoax, Patterson and Gimlin (joined by DeAtley) then reportedly traveled with the film to Universal Studios in Hollywood the week after returning from Vancouver. According to an account offered by the three men from Washington State – there is no independent collaboration of what occurred from the studio – they arranged a meeting with technicians in the Universal special effects department and asked if the moviemakers would be able to duplicate the creature in their film. The studio effects team allegedly claimed that they could not.

In late November, *Life* magazine, the nation's most prominent news weekly, agreed to meet with Patterson, Gimlin, and DeAtley. Whether Patterson made the initial contact or *Life* sought them out is not certain. The magazine paid for the three men to take their film reels to New York with the hopes that *Life* would buy the publication rights to the footage.

But the *Life* editors wanted scientific verification of the film, and arranged for screenings with scientists at the American Museum of Natural History and the Bronx Zoo. The museum screening consisted of a single run-through of the brief footage and the abrupt dismissal of its contents as a hoax. The zoo screening had at least two replays of the footage along with pauses for frame measurements, but the final opinion was negative. With these twin rejections, *Life* opted not to publish the screen captures from the Patterson-Gimlin Film.

However, the trip to New York was not in vain. There was a Plan B waiting for Patterson and Gimlin in the form of Ivan T. Sanderson, the cryptozoologist whose work inspired Patterson years earlier. Sanderson saw *Life*'s rejection as his chance for a major scoop, and he arranged with Harry Steeger, the publisher of a monthly men's-focused magazine called *Argosy*, to investigate the legitimacy of the footage. Sanderson set up a screening of the film in December in Washington, D.C., with a line-up of experts from the Smithsonian Institution, the Department of the Interior, the U.S. Coast and Geodetic Survey. Also in attendance were the editor of *National Geographic*, and two Canadian academicians.

"During a four-hour session, the film and stills were shown, examined under high magnification, challenged, questioned, argued about and studied," Sanderson later wrote. "The scientists did not agree on all points. They did not even all see exactly the same details in the often hard-to-read blowups. But after a careful scrutiny over a period of hours, not one voiced the suspicion that there was a vague possibility that someone with enormous funds, a strange, undecipherable motivation, a disregard for life and limb, and an enormous knowledge of anatomy, physiology, photography and human psychology might have been clever enough to set up a hoax good enough to fool the top experts in the field."

As if to give his effort an extra oomph in selling, Sanderson arranged a special review of the film by Dr. Osman Hill, the director of Emory University's Yerkes Regional Primate Research Center. Hill's response: "All I can say that if this was a masquerade, it was extremely well done and effective." Hill also suggested that the film was solid enough to spur further research into the subject.

With this feedback, *Argosy* agreed to publish screen captures from the Patterson-Gimlin film, along with an article by Sanderson on the men who were responsible for the footage. The story appeared on the cover of the February 1968 edition, with five screen captures of the Sasquatch along with the headline "Exclusive! First Photos! California's Abominable Snowman." Beneath the headline was the subhead that promised, "Gimlin and Patterson: How we found and photographed it."

Also on the cover was a photo of Patterson and Gimlin on horses, along with a third horse used for carrying supplies. That photograph was particularly odd because it offered Gimlin wearing a long black wig and a white headband, which gave the impression he was a 19th century Indian scout rather than a contemporary individual who was only one-quarter Native American. It is not known who came up with the idea of dressing Gimlin in such a theatrical manner.

Sanderson's article offered an eloquent defense against the arguments that the Patterson-Gimlin Film was a hoax. He raised the question of the absence of Sasquatch bones or fossils and challenged the inquiry by claiming: "My answer is to simply go and ask any game warden, real woodsman or professional animal collector if he has ever found the dead body or even the bone of any wild animal—except along roads, of course, or killed by man. I never have, in forty years, in five continents! No. Nature takes care of her own and damn fast too."

Sanderson then wondered aloud about the belief that such a species could remain unknown for so long. He pointed out the discovery of hitherto unknown creatures during the twentieth century, including Cotton's wide-lipped rhinoceros in 1910, the okapi in 1911, the giant sable antelope in 1929, and an Indochina ox called the kouprey in 1956.

Sanderson also took aim at the journalists who failed to support Patterson and Gimlin. "The leading news media—not the working press, I should stress—treated this whole thing as an uproarious joke," he complained, adding that *Argosy* did not share that disbelief. He concluded his piece by proclaiming, "This story is definitely to be continued."

Taking the Act on the Road

However, *Argosy* never returned to the Patterson-Gimlin Film, although Sanderson would author a few additional articles related to the search for the elusive Sasquatch. *Argosy* ceased publication in 1978.

Patterson tried to keep the story active via television appearances without Gimlin on Joe Pyne's syndicated talk show and the late-night talk shows hosted by Joey Bishop and Merv Griffin. Video copies of these appearances are not believed to exist, and it is uncertain if Patterson allowed the footage from Bluff Creek to be broadcast.

In November 1967, Patterson, Gimlin, and DeAtley formed Bigfoot Enterprises, with ownership of the film split between the three. But their plans for marketing the film seemed to be stalling. *National Wildlife* ran an article on the film in its April/May 1968 edition, but no other reputable publication wanted the story.

Patterson hoped to maintain momentum by creating his own documentary on the hunt that led him and Gimlin to their encounter with the mysterious being. Shooting with a 16mm camera, the men were joined by mutual friends in recreating pre-Bluff Creek hunts for the Sasquatch. This went on for three days, but a lack of funds and a perceived lack of commercial viability brought their endeavor to a halt.

Then, the most unlikely intervention happened. The British Broadcasting Corporation (BBC) contacted Patterson with the request to show the Bluff Creek footage on their network. But rather than doing a one-off news item on the film, the BBC actually planned to do a short documentary on the legends surrounding the Sasquatch. The BBC did not pay for the licensing of the footage, but instead offered to provide the Americans with a master copy of their documentary under the provision that it would not be broadcast on U.S. television.

According to Al DeAtley, the BBC footage was spliced together with the unfinished film that Patterson shot plus additional footage, with Sasquatch hunters offering their opinions on the subject. The resulting film was titled *Bigfoot: America's Abominable Snowman* and was presented by Northwest Research Association, another company created by Patterson with the purpose of maintaining interest in the subject of Sasquatch.

Patterson and DeAtley conversed with Ron Olson, an Oregon-based Army veteran whose family ran the American

National Enterprises film distribution company out of Salt Lake City. Olson explained the concept of four-walling, where films were rolled out on a city-by-city basis and theaters were rented out from the exhibitors for a specific time period. Through this method, the distributor received 100 percent of the box office returns, as opposed to having the exhibitor siphon off a share as per the traditional release pattern. In markets where there were no cinemas, high school auditoriums and private clubs that had film projector set-ups were rented out. American National Enterprises had perfected this technique, releasing cheaply-made nature documentaries in smaller markets that were mostly overlooked by the Hollywood distribution networks.

Patterson opted to bring his production out in a limited release pattern aimed at the Pacific Northwest audiences. The marketing for *Bigfoot: America's Abominable Snowman* was loud and exploitative, calling attention to a film "in full color and sound" with the advertised promise: "See Roger Patterson come face to face with a female creature that stood over 7 feet tall. He is the first person to ever film BIGFOOT." Patterson made personal appearances at the cinemas showing his movie, and the poster art featured Patterson mounted on his horse, along with the plaster casts taken from Bluff Creek. The advertisements did not show the imagery of Bigfoot, nor was there any mention of Gimlin's role in the filming of the encounter.

In an interview with researcher Greg Long, Al DeAtley recalled that *Bigfoot: America's Abominable Snowman* premiered at a high school auditorium on a Sunday in Lakeview, Oregon. "Three showings, and every one of them was sold out," he said. "We turned people away. Like, we had 80 percent of the population of the area show up."

DeAtley would later expand on the Lakeview premiere in an interview with Bigfoot researcher Joshua Blu Buhs, recalling that Patterson joined him at their motel in town to count out the box office returns, which were piled into a trashcan. "We were throwing it at each other on the bed and stuff!" he stated.

Of course, it helped that *Bigfoot: America's Abominable Snowman* was heavily advertised in local radio and television stations in advance of its screenings, and it would only play in a single venue in a single locality for one day. "Very high promotion," DeAtley added. "Lots of ads. Total saturation. It was the greatest thing that's ever been, and they've never been hit that hard with advertising before."

But rather than partnering with Olson's American National Enterprises, DeAtley and Patterson thanked him for his insight and went along without his help. "Bullshit on these guys," DeAtley later said about Olson and his family's company. "They'd given me the whole recipe."

In 1968, *Bigfoot: America's Abominable Snowman* played throughout Washington and Oregon. DeAtley estimated that 38 prints of the 96-minute 16mm film were struck. The excessive advertising for the production helped swell interest, and one-day theater rentals were expanded into four-day exhibitions. By 1969, Patterson and DeAtley began expanding their screenings in theaters and schools outside of the Pacific Northwest, taking the film to Idaho, Utah, Colorado, Nebraska, North Dakota, South Dakota, Wisconsin and Minnesota. In nearly all locations, the film was commercially successful and rivaled the box office returns of high-profile Hollywood productions playing on local screens.

As *Bigfoot: America's Abominable Snowman* was being seen by more people, fissures deepened in the relationship between the three men who owned the film. Gimlin, who was increasingly marginalized by Patterson in the marketing of their footage and was initially shut out of receiving any of the profits from the four-walling theatrical endeavor, would recall in a 2016 interview with *Outside* magazine that the Bluff Creek adventure was the worst thing that could have happened to him.

"It ruined me," Gimlin told the magazine, adding that the notoriety had a harsh effect on his marriage. "My wife was a teller at a savings and loan institution. Of course, she was sitting right there and the public would come in and make smart remarks. This went on and on and on until she came home crying. She'd say, 'I'm not tough enough.' A couple times we were going to split over this."

The Gimlins would also be harassed at their home in Yakima. "They'd come driving in my driveway all times of the night and go 'Bob! We want to go out Bigfoot hunting!'" he added.

DeAtley had his own problems with Patterson. In an interview with Greg Long, he remembered Patterson asking him to withdraw from Bigfoot Enterprises in the spring of 1969. DeAtley was eager to return to his life and to leave Bigfoot behind – especially since he did not share Patterson's faith and enthusiasm for the Sasquatch subject.

"I had no interest in it," he said. "I didn't believe in it. It, it, it gnawed at my conscience some. Because if I was ever interviewed or talked to anybody, I had to portray myself as a believer."

DeAtley transferred his ownership rights to the Bigfoot footage to Patterson on August 5, 1970. On that same day, Patterson signed a deal with American National Enterprises, the company that inspired the four-walling of the Bigfoot documentary, which included the sale of the Bluff Creek footage.

This decision was not spontaneous: At the time that Patterson was agitating for DeAtley to exit their venture, he was also in secret talks with American National Enterprises to create a new company called Big Foot Ventures that would serve as the controlling entity of the 1967 encounter film.

A Quest for Legitimacy

While all of this was transpiring, the Bigfoot story was barely receiving any national mainstream media attention. *Reader's Digest* did a very short item on the film in March 1969, and the write-up was included in its international edition, but a serious scientific acceptance of the footage remained elusive – at least in North America.

The Canadian Sasquatch researcher René Dahinden, who was absent from Patterson's foray into film distribution, believed that a new push was needed to get the approval of the scientific community on the subject of the Sasquatch. In his view, any discussion of the topic would be meaningless unless the Sasquatch was seen as a genuine creature and not a hirsute bit of folkloric fun.

Realizing that Patterson had exhausted the good will of the American and Canadian experts who could have given him that elusive seal of approval, Dahinden opted to look elsewhere for validation. At his own expense, he arranged for copies of the Patterson-Gimlin Film and the footprint plaster casts to be made. In 1971, he traveled to Europe, where he sought out academic and anthropological experts and arranged for them to study the footage and the footprint plaster casts.

Dahinden made his way through Great Britain, Finland, Sweden, Switzerland, and the Soviet Union. For the most part, the expert European opinion was not very much different from the indifferent and dismissive nature of the American and Canadian opinion. A respectful judgment was offered by Dr. Donald W. Grieve, an anatomist at London's Royal Free Hospital School of Medicine, who based his observation on the running speed of the film. He noted that "the possibility of fakery is ruled out if the speed of the film was 16 or 18 frames per second. In these conditions a normal human being could not duplicate the observed pattern, which would suggest that the Sasquatch must possess a very different locomotor system to that of man."

However, he added, if the film was shot at the standard 24 frames per second, then the Sasquatch's movements could have easily been recreated by a suited performer and the film had to be seen as a fake. Of course, Patterson's inability to recall how his 16mm camera was set that day only added to the confusion.

Dahinden received a far more welcoming reception behind the Iron Curtain. The Russian Central Scientific Research Institute of Prosthetics and Artificial Limb Construction studied the film at great length and made detailed observations on the movement and muscle mass of the filmed Sasquatch. But this institute stopped short of making a formal conclusion on the film's validity, only releasing a letter to the USSR Committee on Cinematography that recommended the film "contains sufficiently clear frames of the walk of a manlike creature, a detailed study of which would undoubtedly be of serious scientific interest."

More Soviet experts were brought into the mix to study the film. Dimitri Bayanov and Igor Bourtsev, a pair of prominent hominologists, addressed the question of the film's running speed and concluded that it was shot at 16 frames per second. An intense frame-by-frame study led to the identification of similarities between the sole of the Saquatch's right foot and the plaster cast provided by Dahinden. A third Soviet scientist, Dr. Dmitri Donskoy of the USSR Institute of Physical Culture, was also recruited for a professional opinion, and after a long study he announced that the walk "demonstrated by the creature is absolutely non-typical of man."

Unfortunately for Dahinden, his European odyssey failed to shift the credibility needle back home. There was even doubt among cryptozoology thought leaders, including the influential Bernard Heuvelmans, who dismissed the appearance and behavior of the Sasquatch in the film as having no correspondence to any primate species.

Dahinden's efforts were not acknowledged by Patterson, who trying to move beyond Bluff Creek and further the notion of Sasquatches in existence around the West Coast and overseas. In 1969, Patterson tried to raise money for an expedition to Thailand after receiving word that a Sasquatch-type creature had been captured and was being held in a Buddhist monastery. The story was eventually revealed to be a hoax, thus wasting Patterson's time and energy.

An Unhappy Conclusion

And at this point, Patterson had precious little time and energy left. Unknown to everyone but his family and closest friends, Patterson was diagnosed with Hodgkin's lymphoma in the 1960s. The fact that he could maintain a demanding physical schedule and push himself to emotional extremes in his single-minded pursuit of Bigfoot was a testament to his spirit and determination.

But by 1969, his health was beginning to fray and he was unable to complete many personal appearances on the four-walling theatrical release of his film. The financial costs of his health care also created great stress that only exacerbated his deteriorating health.

At the start of 1972, Patterson reached out to Gimlin – the two men had been estranged for the past few years, and Gimlin was initially not enthusiastic about a reunion. But upon learning how badly Patterson's health had declined, he agreed to visit the small home in Tacoma, Washington, where Patterson lived in his final months. The two men reconciled their personal differences.

Roger Patterson died on January 15, 1972. Up until the very end, he always insisted that the film he shot was not faked. His final comment on the subject was a regret that he did not shoot and kill the Sasquatch and return with the body, thus offering irrefutable evidence that he was telling the truth.

After Patterson's death, Gimlin approached his former partner's widow, Patricia Patterson, regarding the failure to provide him with the profits from the screenings of the Bluff Creek film. Unable to settle amicably with Mrs. Patterson, Gimlin filed a lawsuit against her and Al DeAtley in 1974. Gimlin was supported in his efforts by René Dahinden, who published his book *Sasquatch* in 1973 and initially sought out Gimlin to help in its promotion. Dahinden offered to cover Gimlin's legal expenses in exchange for one-half of the one-third of the ownership of the film.

Gimlin's lawsuit ended in his favor in February 1976, when he wound up being rewarded 51 percent of the ownership interest in the Bigfoot footage; Mrs. Patterson retained 49 percent. Gimlin was rewarded 100 percent of all past, present and future publication rights of the imagery connected to the film.

After this ruling, Dahinden convinced Gimlin that they should sue American National Enterprises, which had released its own feature in 1975 called *Sasquatch: The Legend of Bigfoot*. That company, in turn, was suing Sunn Classic Pictures, claiming that it illegally copied the Patterson-Gimlin film for its 1975 film *The Mysterious Monsters*. American National Enterprises and Sunn Classic Pictures amicably settled out of court.

But Dahinden discovered that Roger Patterson had recklessly sold rights to the footage to multiple companies in the U.S. and Canada. Also complicating matters were legal claims made against Roger Patterson's estate by Pat Mason, a friend of Patterson who assisted in promoting the theatrical release of *Bigfoot: America's Abominable Snowman*, and Vilma Radford, another Yakima resident who claimed that Patterson never repaid a loan she made when he was planning the film's release. She also insisted that Patterson promised her five percent of the film's profits.

While Dahinden was eager to use the courts to unravel the confusion, Gimlin grew tired and unhappy with the litigation. In September 1979, Gimlin voluntarily sold his rights to the Bigfoot footage to Dahinden for ten dollars, retaining only one print of the film for his private collection.

Dahinden's legal pursuit of the ownership of the film concluded in March 1982, when the tangle over the multiple rights issuances were settled. Dahinden wound up with 51 percent of the controlling rights to the film footage and 51 percent of home video rights, as well as complete rights to the publication of the 952 frames that made up the Patterson-Gimlin Film. Mrs. Patterson retained 100 percent of television rights and 49 percent of controlling rights to the footage.

But while the legal wrangling was taking place, the Patterson-Gimlin Film was beginning to percolate into the wider popular culture. The editors at *Life* magazine had a change of mind and decided that they wanted to do a story on the film and its elusive subject. However, the magazine was undergoing financial difficulties and ceased publication in late 1972 before its planned coverage was published.

In January 1974, *Smithsonian Magazine* gave the subject a level of scientific respect that that Patterson failed to achieve in his lifetime. The article "The Search Goes on for Bigfoot" referred to a "California rancher named Roger Patterson" as the driving force behind the filmed record of a Sasquatch, adding, "It is unfortunately of very poor quality, taken with a cheap 16-millimeter camera at a distance of more than 100 feet. Worse, Patterson was not sure whether the camera was set at 16 frames per second (fps) or at 24."

The article offered a respectful consideration of the subject, stating "there is currently no proof one way or the other." Nonetheless, having *Smithsonian Magazine* offering the benefit of the doubt to the legitimacy of the footage was a major coup for those advocating that the Sasquatch was a genuine creature, and not the figment of folkloric imagination or the result of excessively creative filmmaking.

And speaking of creative filmmaking, it seemed that the Patterson-Gimlin Film brought forth a new genre: Bigfoot cinema!

A Bigfoot Interlude: Why Did the Sasquatch Cross the Road?

On August 27, 2012, the Associated Press reported the death of a Montana man who was trying scare motorists into thinking he was Bigfoot.

For reasons that will never be understood, 44-year-old Randy Lee Tenley dressed up in a military style "Ghillie suit" that vaguely resembled the popular concept of a Sasquatch, and stood in the right-hand lane of U.S. Highway 93 south of Kalispell. The driver of one car, a 15-year-old girl, did not see Tenley in his dark costume until it was too late, and she ran him over. A second car, driven by a 17-year-old girl, drove over him as he lay in the road.

""He was trying to make people think he was Sasquatch so people would call in a Sasquatch sighting,"" said State Trooper Jim Schneider. "You can't make it up. I haven't seen or heard anything like this before. Obviously, his suit made it difficult for people to see him."

Chapter Four
Bigfoot Cinema

"We have this need for some larger-than-life creature"
– Dr. Robert M. Pyle

Prior to the Patterson-Gimlin Film, the only hominid to dominate the big screen was the Himalayan Yeti. The 1954 B-grade feature *The Snow Creature* offered a thinly disguised retooling of *King Kong*, with a mysterious creature captured in an exotic location and brought back to the United States, where it breaks free from its captivity and creates wreckage and ruin in a big city (in this case, Los Angeles) before being killed. W. Lee Wilder, the none-too-versatile brother of legendary filmmaker Billy Wilder, produced and directed this low-budget quickie, while Oscar-winning cinematographer Floyd Crosby (in something of a career nadir) captured the madness on camera.

Three years later, the Yeti turned up again in the 1957 offering *The Abominable Snowman*. Produced by Britain's Hammer Film Studios, this feature was actually a film version of a 1955 BBC television play called *The Creature*. (Sadly, *The Creature* was broadcast live and never preserved on film, and its only remnants are a few still photographs from the production.) *The Abominable Snowman* (retitled *The Abominable Snowman of the Himalayas* for its U.S. theatrical run) starred American character actor Forrest Tucker and British horror icon Peter Cushing in an odd morality play that pits ruthless and reckless human hunters against a gentle community of placid Himalayan Yeti. The film was unusual because the Yeti were mostly off-camera, and the only significant view of the creature was a close-up of its eyes.

Neither *The Snow Creature* nor *The Abominable Snowman* made any great impact on audiences, and Yeti-themed films ceased until Bigfoot mania began to take root. However, a couple of Yeti-inspired creatures inspired cult followings in early 1960s animated classics. The 1961 Looney Tunes short *The Abominable Snow Rabbit* found Bugs Bunny and Daffy Duck encountering a gigantic talking Himalayan Yeti whose behavior appeared to be modeled on Lon Chaney, Jr.'s characterization of the dimwitted Lenny in the 1939 movie classic *Of Mice and Men*. Another oversized Yeti-type creature turned up in the 1964 television classic *Rudolph the Red-Nosed Reindeer* as the Abominable Snow Monster of the North, with no mention of any previous Himalayan residence or relatives. A Yeti figured in the 1967 second serial of the fifth season of the British science fiction television series *Doctor Who* – sadly, only two of the six episodes of that serial are known to survive.

In the aftermath of the Patterson-Gimlin Film and the attention that Roger Patterson's self-released *Bigfoot: America's Abominable Snowman* had received in the Northwest, the ABC Western series *Here Come the Brides* offered a 1969 episode titled "The Legend of Bigfoot," with the title character portrayed as a white-furred giant. The following year, independent producer Anthony Cardoza figured that he could cash in on the attention generated by the new interest in Sasquatches. Sadly, Cardoza was not the most gifted filmmaker – some of his titles include the infamous stinkers *Night of the Ghouls*, *The Beast of Yucca Flats*, and *Red Zone Cuba* – and his 1970 *Big Foot* affirmed his chronic inability to produce quality entertainment.

Cardoza also set the precedent that has dominated Bigfoot cinema: the seemingly indifferent female Sasquatch walking away from the human intruders behind the camera in the Patterson-Gimlin Film is transformed in movies into a hostile male creature who reacts with physical and, on occasion, sexual violence against the humans who cross his path.

Big Foot offered a confused tale of a lady pilot (Joi Lansing, in her final screen role) who bails out of a malfunctioning airplane, only to be captured on the ground by an erotically aroused Sasquatch. Another woman, the girlfriend of a biker (played by Christopher Mitchum), is also kidnapped by a Sasquatch, and then a third woman is abducted in the same way. The biker is aided by his Harley-riding comrades and a fast-talking traveling salesman (John Carradine) in the rescue of the women – and not a moment too soon, as the Sasquatches were capturing the women with the sole purpose of using them for mating. Obviously, these males Sasquatches were unaware of the female specimen in the Patterson-Gimlin Film.

Big Foot was plagued by the distribution limitations that were common for the low-budget exploitation flicks of the early 1970s, and few people at the time of its release bothered to seek it out. One of the very few prominent individuals to see *Big Foot* and live to tell about it was Pulitzer Prize-winning film critic Roger Ebert, and even he seemed puzzled to be in the theater with this movie on its screen.

"Why, you are asking, did I decide to see *Big Foot*?" Ebert asked. "Why am I taking your time – time you could spend trimming your toenails and talking to your indoor plants, telling them what nice plants they are -- to review *Big Foot*? What strange light in the sky, what weird whistling in my ear, what blood-soaked note tied to a rock and thrown through my window, sent me to see *Big Foot*? These are good questions."

Big Foot remained mostly forgotten until the advent of home video in the 1980s, when it re-emerged as a jolly entry in the so-bad-they're-good niche of cheesy horror romps. Another obscure Bigfoot film of that era emerged from an even less sophisticated corner of the motion picture world: *The Geek* (1971) was aimed at the patrons of the pornographic cinemas and envisioned the carnal encounters between a Sasquatch and two women hiking in the woods. As with *Big Foot*, this film was mostly unknown until it re-emerged in the age of home video.

The next entry in the Bigfoot cinema world made a more provocative impression: The 1972 production *The Legend of Boggy Creek*, did not inspire laughs, but instead offered a glimpse of how a cinematic Sasquatch could create genuine thrills.

The creature in this production was not the Patterson-Gimlin Bigfoot, but the so-called Fouke Monster, a Sasquatch-type creature spotted in Miller County, Arkansas, in the early 1970s. Aspiring filmmaker Charles B. Pierce, who ran an advertising agency specializing in television commercials for regional companies, opted to create a pseudo-documentary on the subject. Pierce recruited purported eyewitnesses to the Fouke Monster and spun recreations of their encounters using nonprofessional actors from Miller County. Pierce brought the film in on a ridiculously small $160,000 budget, but his wonderfully creepy approach attracted the appreciation of drive-in and grindhouse audiences. Released by low-budget Howco International, *The Legend of Boggy Creek* grossed $4.8 million in theatrical rentals, making it the tenth highest grossing film of 1972 – putting it in the company of *The Godfather*, *The Poseidon Adventure*, *What's Up, Doc?*, and the groundbreaking skin-flick feature *Behind the Green Door*. Over the years, the film spawned a number of sequels and rip-offs that never quite matched the visceral shock of the original.

More Sasquatch-themed narrative films turned up in the early 1970s. *Shriek of the Mutilated* (1974) offered a surprise twist in a tale of a college professor who lures students into a hominid hunt: it seems the professor and an accomplice wearing a Sasquatch costume are actually cannibals with a hunger for the young pupils. *Creature from Black Lake* (1976) has Jack Elam as a trapper who is joined by two college students in pursuit of a Bigfoot-type creature. Neither film made much of an impression when released. *Curse of Bigfoot* (1976), despite its name, actually had nothing to do with the hairy hominid; it was an expanded version of an unreleased film from the 1960s about the discovery and resurrection of a mummified corpse.

Sasquatch: The Legend of Bigfoot (1978) offered a dramatized expedition that attempted to locate the creature. That film caught the attention of *New York Times* critic Janet Maslin, who described the title character as "a pointy-headed fellow in a Kong suit, who is seen throwing papier-mâché boulders a few times and whose presence is often represented by 'Jaws'-type music and rustling branches." Maslin added that films of this type represented "the kind of pseudoscientific silliness that manages to discredit itself entirely."

Arguably, the most widely-seen Bigfoot-based drama of this period was a two-part episode on the popular ABC series *The Six Million Dollar Man*, in which Bigfoot (played by professional wrestler Andre the Giant) was a robot created and controlled by aliens. The character proved to be so popular with audiences that it was brought back in a two-part crossover story shared by *The Six Million Dollar Man* and its spinoff *The Bionic Woman*. This time,

Bigfoot was played by Ted Cassidy, the oversized character actor best known as the butler Lurch on the classic sitcom *The Addams Family*. Cassidy reprised the Bigfoot role for a one-shot 1977 episode of *The Six Million Dollar Man*.

While these narrative works were being created, a new fascination by Americans with the paranormal, cryptozoology, and unexplained phenomena began to permeate popular culture. A surprisingly large number of theatrical and television documentaries were turned out to tap into this trend. Some of these productions covered a vast array of funky subjects that included Bigfoot in the merry mix, while others looked solely at the chase for the Sasquatch.

Lawrence Crowley's documentary *Bigfoot: Man or Beast?* (1972) introduced many filmgoers to the Patterson-Gimlin footage, even though Gimlin was conspicuously erased from the narrative. (Patterson was described as being in Bluff Creek "with a friend.") A brief audio interview with Patterson describing the 1967 was included, and Sasquatch researchers including René Dahinden and Grover Krantz are interviewed. However, the bulk of the film focuses on Robert Morgan's expedition into the Mount St. Helens wilderness in search of Bigfoot. Of course, Morgan came up empty, but the film record of his efforts was well-produced and compelling.

Robert Guenette's 1975 *The Mysterious Monsters* opened with actor Peter Graves looking directly at the camera and warning, "Scientists representing the world's most foremost research centers took part in the examination of the evidence. The facts that will be presented are true. This may be the most startling film you'll ever see." Bigfoot shared screen time with the Yeti and the Loch Ness monster in this documentary, which was released in theaters by Sunn Classic Pictures, a Salt Lake City-based distributor specializing in kooky fare including the landmark Oscar-nominated ancient aliens documentary *Chariots of the Gods* and the revisionist historical narrative *The Lincoln Conspiracy*. *The Mysterious Monsters* was broadcast on NBC in prime time in 1977, reaching an even wider audience.

Also in 1977, the popular television series *In Search Of…*, hosted by Leonard Nimoy, debuted. The fifth episode of the first season was devoted to entirely to Bigfoot. That same year saw Tom Biscardi's *In the Shadow of Bigfoot*, a feature-length documentary that includes interviews with people who claimed to have a close encounter of a Sasquatch kind. In 1978, Nicholas Webster's *Manbeast: Myth or Monster?* offered a wider look at elusive hominids, including Bigfoot and the Yeti.

The Bigfoot movie and television mania of the 1970s ended with a fairly mundane narrative feature, *The Capture of Bigfoot* (1979) from low-budget horror veteran Bill Rebane, and one of the weirdest television programs ever conceived: Sid and Marty Krofft's series *Bigfoot and Wildboy*, with the Sasquatch as the adoptive father of a feral youth named Wildboy, who walks around in leather clothing and a shaggy blonde hairdo. (It is unclear where Wildboy got his wardrobe and trendy hairstyling.) This series presented the title characters as unofficial crime fighters, working to keep their forest safe from both human and extra-terrestrial miscreants. Hey, it was the 1970s – for that decade, this was fairly normal.

The 1980s started with another vicious Bigfoot attacking humans in *Night of the Demon* (1980), but then interest in the subject seemed to abruptly evaporate. In 1987, three Bigfoot films were released that transformed the creature from a vicious, homicidal, and sexually ravenous monster into a family-friend bundle of fun who was kind to kids, good for a laugh, and something of a role model.

Jay Schlossberg-Cohen's *Cry Wilderness* imagined the friendship between a talking Sasquatch and a little boy whose father is a California park ranger trying to hunt down a tiger that escaped from captivity and hid in the woods. The film was somewhat under the radar in its initial theatrical run, but later gained a wider audience as the subject of wisecracking ridicule on the *Mystery Science Theatre 3000* cable television show.

A more substantial addition to Bigfoot cinema was *Harry and the Hendersons*. Produced and directed by William Dear, with Steven Spielberg serving as an uncredited executive producer, the film offered a charming comic fantasy about a suburban family that becomes the unlikely benefactor of a Sasquatch being pursued by Bigfoot hunters. The family even goes so far as to give him the chummy name Harry. In the course of his domestic adventures, Harry initially has problems adapting to living in suburbia, but eventually gets used to its protocols, including television viewing. (One scene has Harry laughing uproariously while watching a rerun of the Ronald Reagan movie *Bedtime for Bonzo*.)

With seven-foot-two actor Kevin Peter Hall inside the Bigfoot costume and make-up created by Rick Baker (who won the Academy Award in the Best Make-Up category for this work), *Harry and the Hendersons* reinvented the Sasquatch as a friendly creature who is initially skittish around humans but is eventually able to differentiate between the good-hearted and the nasty types.

While the critics were mostly unimpressed with *Harry and the Hendersons* – some compared it unfavorably to the similarly-plotted Spielberg classic, *E.T. the Extra-Terrestrial* – audiences were happily distracted by the film and made it one of the year's box office hits. The film spawned a syndicated television series that ran for three seasons from 1991 to 1993. The series generated bad reviews in spite of audiences' favorable reaction.

The third Sasquatch feature of 1987 was the made-for-television Disney film *Bigfoot*, directed by Danny Huston. This production centered on two spunky kids and an anthropologist (played by Colleen Dewhurst) who encounter a Sasquatch couple. This film offers a rare example of a female Sasquatch, and it suggests that the creatures are monogamous.

Bigfoot was mostly absent from view in the 1990s. However, some memorable Bigfoot-inspired moments did emerge during this decade. On television, a mud-caked Homer Simpson on a camping trip was mistaken for Bigfoot in the classic 1990 episode of *The Simpsons* "The Call of the Simpsons." The A&E series *Ancient Mysteries* devoted an episode to the subject in 1994, but broke little new ground on the topic.

On the big screen, Bigfoot cinema in the 1990s was scant, but when it did pop up it was mostly mirthful and light fantasy-themed. *Bigfoot: An Unforgettable Encounter* (1994) found the Sasquatch befriending a young boy in the woods – the film's poster featured the child riding happily on Bigfoot's broad shoulders. Disney inserted a jolly Bigfoot into *A Goofy Movie* (1995), with Goofy and his son Max encountering the legendary entity during a camping trip. Another comic presentation was in *Drawing Flies* (1996), produced and financed by indie film icon Kevin Smith, who turns up briefly in his Silent Bob persona. In this film, a group of Canadian slackers winds up in the woods when one of their circle offers them shelter at his uncle's log cabin. Of course, you-know-who shows up. Unfortunately, Smith realized that this black-and-white film was a mess and kept it out of release for years, only putting it on DVD in a barely-publicized 2002 release.

Then there was the direct-to-video feature *Little Bigfoot* (1997), in which a young Sasquatch and his family are threatened by a logging company's reckless deforestation. Enough people must have purchased this title, as the sequel *Little Bigfoot 2: The Journey Home* (1998) found the pint-sized Sasquatch being targeted by a disreputable landowner who tried to capture him and sell him to a circus.

With the dawn of the 21st century, the proliferation of digital video equipment and the Internet enabled anyone to make and release feature-length films cheaply and easily. As a result of these breakthroughs, enterprising would-be filmmakers rediscovered the concept of Bigfoot and a new flood of Bigfoot-inspired films polluted the market.

It would be sadistic to inflict an in-depth consideration of each of the 21st century Bigfoot flicks (not to mention Yeti-inspired movies) on the good people reading this book, so let's acknowledge their existence by listing some of the more salacious and deliciously silly titles of this output: *Squatch on the Rocks!* (2003), *Sasquatch: Legend Meets Science* (2003), *Sasquatch Mountain* (2006), *Abominable* (2006), *Yeti: A Love Story* (2006), *Spotlight on the Patterson-Gimlin Film* (2007), *Bigfoot's Reflection* (2007), *Southern Fried Bigfoot* (2007), *Sesquac: The Story of Sasquatch* (2007), *Sasquatch! A Love Story* (2007), *No Burgers for Bigfoot* (2008), *Not Your Typical Bigfoot Movie* (2008), *Assault of the Sasquatch* (2009), *Yeti: Curse of the Snow Demon* (2008), *Bigfoot Diaries* (2009), *It's a Trip Presents: The Not So Great Sasquatch Hunt* (2009), *Blobsquatch (The Making of Bigfoot X-ing: A*

Documentary) The Documentary (2010), *Bigfoot Is Real!: Sasquatch to the Abominable Snowman* (2010), *Waiting on Sasquatch* (2011), *Le Squatch: Master Criminal* (2011), *Bigfoot's Wild Weekend* (2012), *Bigfoot County* (2012), *Squatch! Curse of the Tree Guardian* (2012), *1313: Bigfoot Island* (2012), *Gingersquatch* (2012), *Shooting Bigfoot* (2013), *Bigfoot Museum* (2013), *SexSquatch* (2013), *Au Coeur de la Forêt du Sasquatch* (2014), *Bigfoot Wars* (2014), *Bigfoot: Curse on the Mountain* (2014), *Oregon: Home of Bigfoot?* (2014), *Bigfoot: The Evidence Files* (2014), *Sasquatch Terror* (2014), *Sorority Sisters vs. Sasquatch* (2015), *Bigfoot in Europe: Sasquatch Encounters Abroad* (2015), *Minerva Monster: Bigfoot of Ohio* (2015), *Bronx Bigfoot* (2016), *Nigel and Oscar vs. the Sasquatch* (2016), *Gimme Head: the Tale of the Cuyahoga Valley Bigfoot* (2016), *Skookum: The Hunt for Bigfoot* (2016), *We Are Sasquatch* (2016), *Bigfoot at Millcreek* (2017), *Son of Bigfoot* (2017), *Suburban Sasquatch* (2017), *Sasquatch on Lake Superior* (2017), *Sasquatch on Lake Superior 2* (2018), *Bigfoot: Blood Trap* (2018), *Bigfoot's Bride* (2018), *Discovering Bigfoot* (2018), *Expedition Sasquatch* (2018) and *Sasquatch I: It Begins – The Curse of the Waresquatch* (2018).

Into the 21st century, references to Bigfoot and appearances by the hominid punctuated numerous television programs, usually in a jokey manner. However, a pair of television programs attempted (with varying levels of success) to give the celebrated Sasquatch some level of serious attention.

In 2014, the cable channel Spike debuted a game show called *10 Million Dollar Bigfoot Bounty*, which pitted nine teams of would-be Sasquatch hunters with the challenge of finding verifiable evidence of Bigfoot's existence in the wilderness. The catch was that the evidence gathered by the teams needed to meet approval of scientific testing – or, at least, the testing set up for the show. The winning team would receive $10 million in prize money.

The series, hosted by actor Dean Cain, was not greeted with any degree of critical admiration. Los Angeles Times critic Patrick Kevin Day wrote that *10 Million Dollar Bigfoot* "hasn't attracted a whole lot of what you would call studious, academic types. Instead, you get a whole lot of angry, sexist rednecks yelling at each other in the woods. What better way to attract a notoriously camera-shy, quite probably mythical creature, than to have a bunch of people arguing in the woods? But it makes for watchable TV."

Well, maybe not that watchable. *10 Million Dollar Bigfoot Bounty* ran for an eight-episode season and was never renewed.

A more lasting television success was *Finding Bigfoot*, which premiered on the Animal Planet cable channel in 2011 and is still, as of this writing, on the air. The episode finds a four-person search team – consisting of Bigfoot Field Researchers Organization founder and president Matt Moneymaker, Sasquatch advocate/researchers James "Bobo" Fay and Cliff Barackman, and Sasquatch skeptical scientist Ranae Holland – attempting to locate evidence to confirm that the Sasquatch exists somewhere in the North American wilderness.

However, as many detractors of the program have tartly observed, a more accurate title for this series might be *Not Finding Bigfoot*, as none of the production's episodes offered any physical, audio, video, or photographic evidence to confirm the existence of this creature. What it offered was unverifiable eyewitness accounts of alleged encounters. Perhaps recognizing that it was building a long-running show on a rather small foundation, the program expanded its focus to hominids in other countries, and episodes would include the hunt for the similar hominids in Australia and Asia, including the now-fabled Yeti.

The *Washington Post* wondered what would happen if the stars of this series actually found Bigfoot. According to Animal Planet General Manager Marjorie Kaplan, the cable network had no contractual arrangement on how to proceed if such a discovery occurred. "But I will tell you when they find Bigfoot, you will know quickly," she said.

The author of this book reached out to Matt Moneymaker for an in-depth interview on the Patterson-Gimlin Film and its impact on popular culture. Alas, Moneymaker did not offer the most cogent or coherent input.

"Although the PGF has been the cornerstone for a few independent films wherein it was presented and discussed, it wasn't a finished film itself — your area of expertise — so I'm wondering why you've taken an interest in it," he wrote in an e-mail. "Are you actually interested in the subject matter? I'm guessing you're the urban type who has probably never met an eyewitness to these creatures, much less had your own encounter, so assumably (sic) you would have no reason or basis for believing they even exist, unless you've seen many documentaries on the subject, which is what got me interested as a kid years before I actually had a face-to-face encounter with one, after 7 years of trying to get that close to one. Anyway, let me know why you've decided to focus on the PGF, which is actually legit, but about which more has already been written and produced than any other piece of footage than perhaps the Zapruder footage. I doubt there's anything new anyone can say about it that hasn't been said ad nauseous (sic) for decades."

A Bigfoot Interlude: Sasquatch vs. E.T.

In the realm of the paranormal, Bigfoot takes a back seat to ancient aliens among Americans who are addicted to the freakier aspects of science.

According to Chapman University's 2017 Survey of American Fears, 55 percent of Americans believe that ancient advanced civilizations, such as Atlantis, once existed, while 52.3 percent believe that places can be haunted by spirits, 35 percent believe aliens have visited Earth in our ancient past, 26.2 percent believe aliens have come to Earth in modern times, and 19.4 percent believe that fortune tellers and psychics can foresee the future.

However, only 16.2 percent believe Bigfoot is a real creature. No explanation was given regarding why Bigfoot's popularity was so minimal.

The Chapman University survey also described the average American who embraced paranormal concepts. "Simply put, the person with the highest number of paranormal beliefs in the United States as of 2017 will tend to be a lower income female living in a rural area in the Western states," the report stated. "She tends to be politically conservative and claims to be highly religious, although she actually attends religious services infrequently. She is either currently single or cohabitating with someone and reports her race as 'other.'"

Chapter Five
Bigfoot or Bigfaux?

For every complex problem there is an answer that is clear, simple, and wrong. – H.L. Mencken

With the dawn of the 21st century, the Patterson-Gimlin Film took on new importance, thanks to digital technology that was used to re-evaluate the footage and to encourage new conversations on what was captured on screen.

A major figure in the digital reconsideration of all things Bigfoot is William Munns, whose 2014 book *When Roger Met Patty* was the result of an intensive seven-year study of the Patterson-Gimlin Film. Munns gained attention for his scientifically inspired model of Gigantopithecus, the prehistoric creature that Sasquatch enthusiasts point to as the predecessor to Bigfoot, and for offering the first digital restoration and analysis of the Patterson-Gimlin Film that enabled a stabilized, high-definition version of the shaky, blurry 16mm film.

"The reason people are still debating the Patterson-Gimlin Film after fifty years is that researchers and critics alike in the past didn't really understand what is necessary to really prove the film true or false, so they created a lot of arguments that ultimately didn't resolve the question," said Munns. "By not resolving it, they intensified the debate. There are, of course, people on both sides of the argument who feel that it's totally solved, but they rely on the false proofs of old as if they were correct. So, most of the argument comes from false ideas, and this confuses the general public and mainstream media. But part of the reason the debate is so strong is that the film itself is so powerful as evidence. There is simply no other encounter or photographic material associated with the bigfoot/sasquatch phenomenon which is anywhere near as powerful as the film. That unique power fuels the debate."

For his part, Munns is not convinced that the footage is fraudulent. "When I personally look at the Patterson-Gimlin Film, I try over and over again to see evidence of the film being faked, and it simply is not there," he continued. "And because I cannot find any evidence of anything fake, I end up seeing something real, something which will eventually change the world of physical anthropology by adding a new hominid to the human family tree."

Munns also noted that the original problems with the film's cinematography give it more credibility than its detractors are willing to admit. "Actually, if the film were made with better camerawork and a most polished effect, that would most likely increase the suspicion about the film being hoaxed, because such a polished effect would raise the suspicion of why people with better equipment just happened upon such a creature," he insisted. "But a man with a simple hand-held 16mm camera, filming as he runs to chase the creature, is the best one could ever expect in real life for such an encounter. The funny thing about the film is that it is commonly described as grainy, shaky and low resolution, but the actual analysis of the film image integrity, frame by frame, dispels that common assumption. The film has remarkable photographic image data useful for analysis, if one simply has the training and knowledge of 16mm film and camerawork, and has access to the 4K high resolution scans of the various copies of the film existing today."

Munns' footage can be seen on YouTube, along with a seemingly endless number of Bigfoot-related videos. Elsewhere on the Internet, social media sites including Facebook and Reddit have numerous forums where Bigfoot devotees share their thoughts, while a variety of blogs, online magazines, and podcasts take the subject to greater depth.

"First and foremost, when I look at the Patterson-Gimlin film, I see something alive and moving with efficiency," said Mark Matzke, co-host of the Bigfoot-oriented podcast *SasWhat*. "I see something that is foreign to my normal experience; it looks like no animal I have ever seen, nor does it look to me like a human being in a 60's-era gorilla costume. I can still get goosebumps watching this footage, because as a child of the late 70's and early 80's, I had read numerous Bigfoot books that mentioned the Patterson-Gimlin Film. But it took me a relatively long time to actually see it – and, despite my childhood fascination with the subject, I will admit to being a bit frightened by what I saw when I finally saw it. I suppose that may help explain the ongoing mystique of this footage. Not only was it obtained in a location and at a time that is quintessential for Bigfoot enthusiasts, but it also provides a striking visual image that one can associate with sighting reports, where before one had to rely on witness sketches or imagination. So, another way to answer the question would be to say: when I look at the footage, I see a living legend striding beside Bluff Creek."

Matzke added that continued online appeal of Bigfoot is helped by the lack of concrete evidence that the film is a hoax. "I think we are still talking about the Patterson-Gimlin Film because no one has yet produced a 'smoking gun' that proves it false," he continued. "There have, of course, been claims of 'I was the man in the suit,' but all that would be needed to stop the conversation is the suit itself. Even a definitive behind-the-scenes picture of it would slam the door on the film. To my knowledge, 'producing the suit' hasn't happened."

A Hoaxing We Will Go?

However, the Patterson-Gimlin Film is not without its detractors. Over the past two decades, a pair of intriguing theories regarding the parties behind the hirsute hominid on camera has percolated: one involving an Oscar-winning make-up whiz, the other involving a pair of less stellar individuals with a compelling story to tell.

First, let's start with the Hollywood connection. In the summer of 1996, Mark Chorvinsky published an article in *Strange Magazine* that offered the most usual theory on the genesis of the Sasquatch in the Patterson-Gimlin Film. In his article, Corvinsky chased down what he claimed was a long-percolating theory that celebrated Hollywood make-up artist John Chambers created a furry simian-type costume which Patterson and Gimlin used for their footage.

How did John Chambers get into the mix? Well, during the 1950s and 1960s, Chambers was one of the most prolific make-up artists in the entertainment industry. His works were seen on the big screen in such features as *Around the World in 80 Days* and *The List of Adrian Messenger*, and on television in several classic series including *The Outer Limits*, *The Munsters* and *Star Trek*. Chambers was best known for creating the innovative simian make-up for the 1968 science-fiction classic *Planet of the Apes*, for which he was given a Special Achievement Academy Award. (There was no Best Make-Up category in the Academy Awards until 1981, and the only other time that the Academy singled out a make-up artist to honor was for William Tuttle's work in the 1964 fantasy *7 Faces of Dr. Lao*.)

But there are several holes in this theory. For starters, there is no evidence that Chambers knew Patterson and Gimlin – nor should they have been acquainted, considering the very different worlds they occupied. No documentation has surfaced to suggest that the men were acquainted. Also, Chambers was heavily involved during the first eight months of 1967 in the planning and production of *Planet of the Apes*, so there would have been very little time for him to pause to construct a simian-style costume for a pair of amateur filmmakers in the northern California woods.

However, Chambers was briefly affiliated with filmmaker John Landis, who had a bit part in the 1970 feature *Beneath the Planet of the Apes* and who recruited Chambers to play a small role in his feature film directing debut, *Schlock* (1971). Make-up artist Rick Baker created the ape-like monster Schlockthropus for Landis' production, and Chorvinsky theorized it was during the production on this film that Chambers admitted his role to Baker that he was responsible for the Patterson-Gimlin Bigfoot costume.

Chorvinsky also quoted make-up artist John Vulvich on how Chambers' supposed work wound up at Bluff Creek. "Patterson could not have afforded to have it scratch built," he said. "I can't imagine that someone like Patterson would have whatever a suit like that would have cost back then – I'm sure it would have been at least in the tens of thousands. He could have rented it, though. He probably called Chambers to rent a suit. I get calls from people all the time who want to rent something from me. I can see someone like Chambers renting it to someone for a grand or something and maybe redoing it some and taking the head off another thing. That was my guess just seeing it."

One year after the Corvinsky article was published, John Landis was quoted in an interview with writer Scott Essman that the Sasquatch in the Patterson-Gimlin Film was connected to Chambers' make-up laboratory. "That famous piece of film of Bigfoot walking in the woods that was touted as the real thing was just a suit made by John Chambers," Landis said.

Chorvinsky attempted to reach Chambers, who was in the twilight of his life at the time and residing in a nursing home. The public affairs representative for the facility passed along the message to Chorvinsky that Chambers said he did not design a costume for the Patterson-Gimlin Film. Separately, writer Bobbie Short managed to interview Chambers at his nursing home, and he expressed amusement over the story.

"Mr. Chambers did say (in regards to the Patterson footage) that he and his crew wished they had done it, because they would have done it differently," Short wrote. "I believe his exact words were, jokingly, 'We could've done better.'"

Chambers passed away in 2001. Oddly, many of the obituaries highlighting his career included the rumored and refuted Bigfoot connection.

A somewhat more plausible hoax theory was first uncovered by writer Greg Long, who interviewed a rodeo rider acquaintance of Patterson and Gimlin named Bob Heironimus in 2001.

"It was in July or August of 1967," Heironimus told Long. "Gimlin said that Robert was going to make a film, and they needed someone to wear a suit. I'm not positive if he used the word 'Bigfoot' or not at the time. Gimlin said, 'He needs someone pretty good size to get in the suit.' I weighed probably one hundred and ninety pounds then. I was six feet tall and as strong as a bull, and I guess I was what they were looking for."

Heironimus described the suit as being made from horsehide and consisting of three parts: legs, a mid-section, and a head.

He estimated the weight of the suit was between twenty and twenty-five pounds, and said it had a foul odor. Heironimus had a handshake agreement with Patterson to be paid $1,000 for his on-camera appearance in the costume. Heironimus borrowed his mother's car to drive to and from the film site in California, and also took credit for being the individual who mailed the footage to Al DeAtley, which he did while Patterson and Gimlin supposedly made fake Bigfoot tracks for their film. Long also interviewed Heironimus' mother, Opal Heironimus, who confirmed seeing the Bigfoot suit in the trunk of her car; Heironimus' nephew, John Miller, also claimed to have seen the suit. Patterson and Gimlin retrieved the suit, according to the Heironimus account, after they returned from Bluff Creek.

However, Heironimus offered no documented or photographic evidence of being with Patterson and Gimlin at Bluff Creek. Long briefly interviewed Gimlin, who denied Heironimus' presence when they shot the film.

But the man-in-the-suit theory was backed by Philip Morris, the owner of a North Carolina theatrical costume company. Morris told Long that he advertised for mail order customers and was contacted by Patterson, who bought a gorilla suit used for the film for $335. Morris said Patterson paid for the suit a with a postal money order; but Morris did not have a receipt to document the transaction. Morris also stated that Patterson quizzed him on how to make the suit's arms longer and how to hide the human eyes behind the gorilla mask.

But Morris would claim his costume was a one-piece outfit with a zipper up the back, and that it was made from artificial fur. This contradicts Heironimus' recollection of the Sasquatch costume he supposedly wore. Morris would also claim that the face of the Patterson-Gimlin Sasquatch was not one of masks from his gorilla costume, nor did his costume come with the floppy breasts that were seen on the creature in the footage.

Morris and Heironimus appeared together in a 2005 National Geographic television special, where Heironimus attempted to recreate the Bigfoot walk while wearing an ape-like costume. Both men were featured in the 2012 Bigfoot debunking documentary *Hoax of the Century*, but filmmaker Tom Biscardi stated that reaction to the film by Bigfoot enthusiasts was so hostile that he eventually withdrew it from sale on Amazon and other e-commerce sites.

"I got so much flack and became tired of hearing people saying, 'Oh, you're full of shit and yada yada yada," Biscardi recalled, adding that he found it impossible to debate those who insist Bigfoot is real. "It's like a cult. That's the situation – it's a frigging cult!"

A Bigfoot Interlude: I'm Bigfoot!

In August 2017, a Bigfoot sighting in the hills of North Carolina was revealed to be something very different from the celebrated Sasquatch: it turned out to be a self-declared shaman having a spiritual communion with the elusive beast.

Gawain MacGregor stated that he was wandering through the forest while wearing hair-covered animal skins. MacGregor, a Minnesota native on holiday in the South, said he was participating in a "sacrament" while gathering emotions and ideas for his blog on "the divine nature of Sasquatch." He added that his animal skin suit and "Sasquatch prayer" recitations enabled him to have several encounters with the legendary hominid, although he declined to give specifics about what took place in these encounters.

"It feels like it brings me closer to nature," he said.

Chapter Six
Cinematic Appreciation

"I am a camera with its shutter open, quite passive, recording, not thinking."
— Christopher Isherwood

In the half-century since it was first shown, the Patterson-Gimlin Film has been studied by almost every expert scientific profession from anthropologists to zoologists. However, the film had never been critiqued by filmmakers and film scholars.

For this chapter, a number of prominent cinema-focused critics, scholars, and creative artists were asked to look at the Patterson-Gimlin Film and offer their views on what they saw in that now-notorious footage. After all, Roger Patterson wanted to be a filmmaker, so why not posthumously welcome him into the profession and set up a peer review?

Kevin Zimmerman

Kevin Zimmerman is a former editor of Variety *and former U.S. editor of* Music Business International.

My first encounter with the Zapruder film of the cryptozoology world came at what was probably just the right time: I was an 11-year-old who, like his schoolmates, was unduly fascinated by the possibility that Man Was Not Alone on this planet.

The "proof" took a variety of shapes. There was Erich von Däniken's *Chariots of the Gods?*, published in 1968 -- a mere year after the making of the PGF! – which was still selling well in paperback. There were the usual Loch Ness monster sightings from across the pond. And there was the then-current release of 1972's "horror docudrama" *The Legend of Boggy Creek*, featuring a distinctly Sasquatchian figure, already well on its way to earning a reported $25 million on a $100,000 budget.

Surely all this, along with such TV movie fare as the UFO-themed *The Disappearance of Flight 412* and *The Devil's Triangle* – combining the Bermuda Triangle, demonic possession, and the immortal Doug McClure – proved beyond a doubt that there were unearthly, possibly sinister forces at work all around us.

But there was certainly something singular about the PGF. The shakiness of the camerawork, the gasp-inducing sight of the Bigfoot turning its indistinct face to the camera and nonchalantly failing to break stride as it continued on its way into the woods … even if you laughed at it (and my friends and I certainly did), there was still the undeniable thrill of "what if?"

Yet even with the distinct lack of Hollywood production values – or even Doug McClure – could you *really* bring yourself into believing what you were seeing? Didn't the Yeti-in-question look a little too much like some big guy wearing an ape suit? Why was such an elusive creature so blasé about being seen? And what was with the perfectly timed turn to the camera? If Sasquatch had been wearing a Stetson and tipped it to the viewer, it would barely have been more laughable.

As I entered my teens I dismissed the PGF as a fairly crude attempt at a hoax, and even though I was impressed by *Close Encounters* I gave a pass to the likes of NBC's *Project U.F.O.* Not even 1977's *Return to Boggy Creek* – wherein no less a personage than *Gilligan's Island*'s Dawn Wells encountered the would-be fearsome beastie – held a camp value for me. To me, Mistah Bigfoot – he dead.

And yet, while von Däniken and the *Boggy Creek* saga have faded from view, Nessie and Bigfoot remain. The reason is, I think, that same childlike desire – hardly limited to actual children – to believe in the otherwise unknown. It's why we still give ourselves over to *The Babadook* and *Stranger Things*, and to a lesser extent the returns of *Twin Peaks* and *The X Files* – whose second feature film was of course subtitled "I want to believe."

Sure, you can make your own Patterson-Gimlin Film with an iPhone and your mom's faux-fur coat, but there's still no beating the original for sheer weirdness. We still want to believe. And if that means heading to YouTube to watch a grainy, 50-year-old clip filmed by a couple of Bigfoot believers and allowing our imaginations to run wild?

So much the better.

Anders Runestad

Anders Runestad is a freelance writer living in the Midwest (www.runestadwrites.com). His book I Cannot, Yet I Must *documents the making of* Robot Monster, *a 1953 movie featuring an actor in a gorilla suit that is supposed to be a robot from outer space.*

The Patterson-Gimlin Film could be summarized as a short clip of what is either a hairy biped or a human in a suit pretending to be one. But the creature aspect of the film is not as central to understanding its impact as it first seems.

Imagine the same footage but replace Bigfoot with a human being, and not a particularly threatening human, either. Not a large, abnormally tall male, not walking in bloodstained clothing, wearing a mask, or swinging around a blade or blunt object. Just any ordinary person strolling along from the same perspective, wearing any ordinary combination of blue jeans, shorts, button-down or t-shirt, or such outdoor gear as hiking boots. This person might be wearing Under Armour for showy athleticism, or whatever was available at the local Target or Wal-Mart, perhaps with sunglasses or carrying a bag.

Whatever the details, the figure enters the frame from the left, exits on the right, and—most importantly—turns to face the camera for a brief, enigmatic moment before facing forward again. And then this person merely walks away in a continuing, purposeful stride. Unconcerned, uninterested, and not running.

Now, does removing Bigfoot and putting an ordinary person in the same context make for a boring film clip?

Less mysterious, surely, and lacking the emotional pull of seeing what may be a creature that science has not discovered.

But the imaginary non-Bigfoot remakes of Patterson-Gimlin that readers conjure in their brains will, in many cases, still stir up fascination, mystery, unease, or a sense of dread. Because without Bigfoot, the overall staging and structure of this brief movie remain identical. And approaching it in this context explains much about why the film obsesses so many.

The film's point-of-view is that of sneaking around and observing, of capturing something unaware that it is being watched while it is being watched. This is not a highly technical trick that requires any great finesse with camerawork or editing. It is not the kind of thing that film school types discuss at length. But this sneak POV is a consistently effective filmmaking trick with a great pedigree.

While *The Exorcist* came preloaded in 1973 with shock moments straight from the novel, William Friedkin was still frequently subtle in how he stirred up audience unease. Among the film's less obvious sources of fear is an uncomfortable motif of introducing characters from behind or the side. What worked for revealing Max von Sydow in *The Exorcist* worked for revealing Bigfoot half a decade before in the Patterson-Gimlin Film.

But the key moment is of course summed up by the frequently reproduced "Frame 352." Bigfoot turns, the watched becoming the watcher and staring straight into the eyes of future decades of viewers. And this breaking the fourth wall is a perfect formula for making viewers jump, particularly in the precise style of old Hollywood movies. Remember an unnerving moment in Alfred Hitchcock's *Rear Window*. Raymond Burr as the creepy neighbor realizes that he is being watched and looks into the camera, giving the audience a shock as good as that felt by James Stewart's immobilized hero. For breaking the fourth wall is the moment that ends the illusion of comfortably watching a scene play out before one's eyes. The subject becomes another spectator and makes the audience feel viewed.

And this is the essence of why the Patterson-Gimlin Film energizes both supporters and skeptics: the film occurs from an initially safe vantage point which is then violated to supply the viewer with an emotional jolt.

If the film is a fake, it is a well-made fake, more intelligently planned than its rudimentary look would suggest. This is precisely why skeptics do not believe in it: it *is* an effective little glimpse of what appears to be borderline alien life. The skeptic side will interpret their emotional thrill as evidence of a ruse, while the Bigfoot believers will continue to feed on it with hope. The way in which it plays out ensures this fascination as much as the subject itself.

In the end, the opinion of this or that anatomist or makeup artist may not matter that much. For if one is going to endlessly obsess over alleged Bigfoot footage, this is exactly what that footage should look like. These are the qualities that make it a uniquely glass half full or empty experience, perfectly suited to polarize believers and skeptics forever.

Jeffrey Peters

Jeffrey Peters is publisher and editor of The News and Times, an online publication highlighting the media and popular culture. He also writes on religion for Maryland's Carroll County Times.

The Patterson-Gimlin capture of a supposed Bigfoot creature is not evidence of the existence of any cryptozoological being, but a manifestation of a primal desire for wonder in the universe. In general, there are three types of people who would respond to this footage: those who believe in a Bigfoot existing and this being one, those who believe in a Bigfoot existing and this not being one, and those who refuse to accept such a creature could exist.

Of the first two types of people, acceptance of the footage can possibly be divided based on the viewer's acceptance of how the Bigfoot creature acts. The creature depicted within the film demonstrates neither aggressive nor truly xenological properties, combining benevolent characteristics of many common animals with a primitive type of humanity. Its body language is casual, as if it is strolling, and the direction of its movement emphasizes its removal from contact. This suggests a level of shyness that is not based on an excited, emotional response (e.g. panic or fear) but on a more rational level of understanding. It does not "flee" because it does not see us as a threat, which helps the viewer to empathize with it, preventing us from seeing it as a threat.

Thus, those who believe that the creature is real most likely accept an optimistic understanding of the universe, one in which humanity and nature can come together. At the same time, those who disbelieve the film are most likely rejecting the casual nature of such a creature, determining that a Bigfoot must be a monstrous being if it exists.

In terms of phenomenology, each person has a preconceived understanding of what Bigfoot should be, whether monstrous or benevolent. A cryptozoological creature is, in all normal aspects, an "other," but a Bigfoot is an "other" that has deep connections to humanity. Such a creature, a less developed cousin of homo sapiens, can represent our more primitive aspects, and these feelings could reflect an individual's view of humanity in general.

As for the third type of people, skeptics who are unwilling to accept the existence of such a creature, their opinions are most likely due to defects in their imagination. Their rational mind has limited the possibility of a Bigfoot regardless of the evidence, seeking other explanations to calm any disturbances that the images may create. This is not a negative, *per se*, but it reveals a level of mental defensiveness that can hinder their acceptance if incontrovertible proof is obtained. Such individuals may never accept that Bigfoot exists even if such a creature began to live with them, as in *Harry and the Hendersons*. The phenomenological aspects of their brain have shut off any possibility of such a creature existing.

Those of the first two types show a willingness to believe in something beyond that which is "factual" in a raw sense. They allow their imaginations to explore possibilities, thus allowing them to accept new ideas if they conform in some degree to what their imaginations already reveal. This is a predisposition to wonder, to seeking something more in the universe.

In this sense, we can separate the first two types from the third in a cultural manner, and it is clear that society has progressed along the line of strict "scientism" and "rationality" since the 19th century that does not allow for wonder or the imagination. Although many, including Werner Heisenberg, expressed the need for science to be open to new ideas and to accept philosophical systems that allow for wonder, many have turned to cold rationality to provide a defense against the unknown.

It is possible that those of the third type were once of the second type, seeing all "others" as monsters, which led to them closing their minds as a defense mechanism. They do not want to believe because to welcome the possibility of such creatures existing could force them to explore other, darker ideas. To see humanity as alone and in control of the universe is to banish feelings of weakness or smallness. It is a comfort, but a false comfort prompted by anxiety over honest desire. Yet our age of cold rationality is also one of great anxiety.

The film, as a whole, reveals the mind of the audience. On its face, it can do little to truly confirm or deny the existence of a Bigfoot, but it provides enough to spark the imagination and fuel speculation on the issue.

Troy Howarth

Troy Howarth is author of the books So Deadly, So Perverse: 50 Years of Italian Giallo Films (Volumes 1-3), Splintered Visions:

The Films of Lucio Fulci, The Haunted World of Mario Bava, *and* Real Depravities: The Films of Klaus Kinski.

When filmmakers Roger Patterson and Bob Gimlin set out to make a documentary about the so-called Bigfoot (or Sasquatch), they knew they would have to "fake" the footage if necessary, in the interests of telling a good story on film. To hear them tell it, however, on the afternoon of October 20, 1967, fate decreed that they would manage to capture some footage (less than a minute, but still!) of a real, live Sasquatch.

Or so they claimed.

But was it real? Or was it just a hoax? In a sense, the fascination with mythical creatures like the Sasquatch is almost a religion unto itself: if you're inclined to believe, then you'll likely accept the grainy, amateurish-looking 16mm footage credible as proof; if you're a skeptic, well…

Perhaps it is due to the artlessness of the footage that it seems so very compelling for some viewers; if it had been filmed with a more aesthetic sensibility, it would be easier to dismiss it as a fake – don't forget, some people still believe that Stanley Kubrick helped NASA to fake the moon landing, after all.

The need to believe in… something… anything… is key to man's existence. Through the years, ideologies and dogmas have been created to provide some sense of meaning in what otherwise can appear a threatening, random, even pointless universe. Is it any wonder, then, that people want so very badly to believe in creatures like the Sasquatch? If it can be proved to exist, then it opens the door to a wide array of possibilities – of mysteries barely concealed from view, obfuscated by society's need for the pragmatic and the logical.

As a confirmed skeptic, I firmly identify with those who are less-than-convinced by the footage captured by Patterson and Gimlin. And yet, there's that part of me – however small – that is willing to be convinced. In that respect, I suppose I can be seen as agnostic rather than doggedly atheistic. I can't count the number of times I have viewed this infamous footage. I can say that when I first saw it, at an impressionable young age, it seemed compelling; seen today, it's admittedly less so.

As such, what I find even more fascinating is the fervent belief and unshakable faith exhibited by those who do accept it as it was presented by its makers. The vaguely moth-eaten looking "creature," staggering through a wooded landscape, crudely captured by a cameraman who appears to be in the midst of a massive panic-attack (or looking to simulate a massive disturbance, Star Trek-style!), continues to capture the imagination. Yes, the fact that it looks so crude makes it look more realistic on the one level, and when that *cinéma vérité* quality is coupled with a sincere (perhaps naïve, depending on one's point of view) desire to believe, it is all the more potent and persuasive.

To less-sympathetic eyes, it could almost appear to be outtakes from the then-latest Toho monster spectacular, with a Japanese extra laconically strolling to his trailer between takes of smashing toy miniatures of Tokyo. As such, it's easy to mock those who cling to it as an anthropological artefact – but at the risk of sounding hopelessly wishy-washy, can any of us put our hand on our heart and state, categorically and with absolute certainty, that there is and indeed never has been such a creature as the Sasquatch? I know I can't.

As for Roger Patterson and Bob Gimlin – Patterson the believer, Gimlin the skeptic who was along for the ride – they would be derided as charlatans by one side, while the other would embrace them for having finally provided concrete evidence of the apparently unbelievable. No matter which side of the fence you may come down on, one thing is for sure: the footage would earn them notoriety and immortality. And sometimes, dear readers, that's more than enough.

Ron Bonk

Ron Bonk is a filmmaker specializing in low-budget/high-imagination horror and science-fiction, including The Vicious Sweet *(1997),* Strawberry Estates *(2001),* Clay *(2007) and* She Kills *(2016). He is the executive producer on the Bigfoot-inspired comedy* SexSquatch *(2003) and is the founder of the B-Movie Film Festival and B-Movie.com website.*

Though the Patterson-Gimlin Film doesn't have the same impact today as it once did for me, it still can be a bit shocking to watch. That may be partially attributed to memories of seeing it first as a child, most likely on *In Search Of...*, but also the documentary style of it. I'll address each individually to better explain.

You have to understand, when I first saw this footage, somewhere in the ballpark of seven or eight years old, I had never seen anything like it. Most of the world hadn't. There were documentaries for sure, but I mostly had not been exposed to them. There were semi-found footage movies like *Cannibal Holocaust* that I had not been exposed to. I didn't often watch the evening news that was exposing horrific scenes of the Vietnam War to America. But where war was something far away or long ago or I had only seen in John Wayne movies, seeing a "monster," footage that looked like a living, breathing animal, for real (or what I believed was real) really marked me in a way I hadn't experienced before. This wasn't presented to me as fiction. This was real (seemingly so at the time, especially to an impressionable child), and the camera person had caught proof that there was much more to our world than I, we, knew about.

People weren't being hit just by Bigfoot, but there were other things emerging from the depths both within and outside the world at this time. I was confronted with a reality that those in charge, the government, my parents, teachers, etc. didn't know "everything" or had not told us "everything." The world wasn't cut and dried / black and white, something that would become glaringly more and more obvious year after year that followed.

Sure, I may certainly doubt the authenticity of footage more every day, but the Patterson-Gimlin Film, among other evidence, opened my brain to the idea that - to borrow in spirit from *The X-Files* - "The truth was still out there." And it would never, even over hundreds of lifetimes, be fully revealed to me, to anyone.

The amateur aspect has certainly been watered down due to so many found footage movies that have come out, myself being among the very first to utilize that style for a feature length movie (with *Strawberry Estates* shot first back in late 1996). But there's something about home movies shot in the actual period – as opposed to ones shot today made to look like decades earlier.

There's an extra element that's harder to put your finger completely on, and may just be a combination of two things: a) the time period, though it can be duplicated, has a feel that no set designer can fully mimic; and b) the film stock, though it certainly can be found and used today, it still seems to lack something when shot and developed in present day.

Then there are a lot of small factors to consider, like how the person behind the camera shot it as opposed to how someone today may frame it up (the camera phone has certainly changed how people capture the world for their memories). But there's something else to it, something in the rawness, grittiness of the footage, maybe burned in invisibly, that hits me and others subconsciously and just makes the footage more effective for today's viewer. It's like how 70's New York City movies have that look that can't be duplicated no matter what measures are taken by modern filmmakers – e.g. film stock, cameras used, set design, developing techniques. It's never quite 100 percent convincing.

And even as I break it down and try to explain it here, I find myself struggling with the right words. It's a feeling, that's all I can say, that I can't verbally or in print form put into proper order and detail, at least not to the extent that I'm satisfied I've properly explained my point. It is sort of that "you had to be there" thing, something that holds true as much as me trying to relate to a child who grew up during World War II or some other key moment in history. I can detail it, a better writer can describe it, and readers or listeners can relate, sympathize, associate, think they identify or emulate, but they don't truly feel it because they weren't there to experience it when it unfolded. If you were there when the footage first hit the public consciousness then you'd better understand why it took hold then and still has an impact on those viewers, no matter what our belief system has formed it into today.

Antero Alli

Antero Alli is an underground filmmaker – The Drivetime *(1995),* Tragos *(2001),* Hysteria *(2002),* Under a Shipwrecked Moon *(2003) and* The Book of Jane *(2016) – and theatrical producer whose work plumbs the protocol of spirituality, interpersonal communications, and the quest for self-identity within a wider and often hostile world.*

Watching the 1967 Patterson-Gimlin footage, I'm not thinking about whether Sasquatch is real or not. I'm thinking about why and how this image - of a giant, hairy, human ape-like forest figure - has magnetized a subculture of obsession over the last fifty years. How did this Bigfoot image become so iconic? I say "image of Bigfoot" because that's what everyone is reacting to: an image. Nobody knows for sure if it's an actual undiscovered species of the wilderness, even though Bigfoot fanatics rant with unwavering certainty that it exists as sure as the Sun Absolute exists.

What is the appeal of this brief video clip? More to the point, what is it about the idea and the image of Bigfoot that has captured the imagination of so many? At some point, we must ask ourselves: what does this monstrous figure of the dark woods represent? Perhaps Bigfoot echoes our lost primordial essence, the feral ancestral soul buried deep in the Collective Unconscious of the domesticated apes of modern civilization. Are those who wander the forests in search of

Sasquatch really seeking their own salvation? Some kind of soul-retrieval ritual, an initiation to the primordial, a restoration of wholeness?

It doesn't matter whether Bigfoot exists or not. There's something bigger at play here. This amateur shaky camera footage has stimulated and maintained a cultural phenomenon of the Imagination. It has taken hold during an era of widespread imagination death sustained by the hard-boiled, over-literalist thinking dominating consensus reality – in the collective mindset, our education systems and mass media. The idea of Bigfoot matters far more than its existence as an undocumented species. It's the myth of Bigfoot that has captured the collective imagination.

I'm seeing Bigfoot as an authentic modern myth – but not a myth as defined and dismissed by the literalists, as in, "it's not true; it's just a myth." Myths and their mythologies have given people meaning and purpose for thousands of years – note the Chauvet cave walls of southern France depicting stick figure paintings of gods and goddesses, battles between great beasts and men, animated and dancing, illuminated by the constant flicker of hearth fires; the first movie - the primordial cinema.

Michael Legge

Michael Legge is a writer/director/actor whose canon – including Working Stiffs, The Dungeon of Dr. Dreck *and* My Mouth Lies Screaming *– specializes in horror-comedy productions.*

I was a weird kid. I grew up during the '50s and '60s and I am what you would call one of the original monster boomers. From the age of six I started watching horror films and science-fiction films, but as I got older I became more interested in what is now called paranormal phenomena. During the '60s there was and still is a magazine called *Fate* which features all sorts of very strange but true paranormal stories. I bought a copy of the magazine way back when, and on the cover was a still picture of a frame from the famous Patterson-Gimlin Film. That was the first time I became aware of its existence. I was still a little kid, but I was looking at it in fascination wondering if it could be true.

Now I'm up in the air about it although I really resent the professional skeptics' knee jerk reaction to dump on anything that doesn't fit into their mindset. It was many years later when I got to actually see the Patterson-Gimlin Film. Granted it's only a few seconds where you can actually make out anything; the camera is initially very jumpy, but there was something about it that was compelling and didn't immediately say fraud to me.

If this footage was taken now from a digital camera it would automatically be considered a hoax and that the creature was CGI or whatever. Unfortunately, digital has harmed any attempts at proving authenticity in terms of the paranormal because it's so easy to fake anything nowadays. You get pretty much skeptical of everything you see.

I do give more credence to anything that was shot on motion picture film, such as 16mm. In that time, unless you were part of a major film studio, there wasn't all that much in terms of special effects that an amateur could do.

It also doesn't look like some costume rental to me. If a suit was made, it was professional job, which would mean big bucks. Why would anyone waste money for a hoax other than wanting attention? You can see in its movements the shining of what appears to be its rippling muscles as it lopes off, which tends to give it even more authenticity.

Over the years there has been a lot of examination of the film frame by frame, minute by minute, and as usual you have the "us versus them" mentality. A lot of the scientific mainstream community doesn't bother to examine the evidence. They'll just say it's fake and dismiss it.

Something to take into account is back in the fossil records there was such a thing as a giant apelike creature named Gigantopithecus, which is said to have been as tall as 8 to 10 feet. The locomotion of the animal is in question, but some experts think it may have been bipedal. Considering that some things exist that we thought were extinct, like the Coelacanth, could some of these giant apes still be hanging around somewhere? It wasn't until the early 2000s that an image of a live giant squid was taken.

The other old argument is that "how come no one has found a dead Bigfoot?" Anybody who lives near a forest, or hikes through them frequently, knows the likelihood of finding a dead deer, bear, or even squirrel is practically nil. The forest is the great recycling plant; small and large predators immediately feed on any carcasses and they are gone quite quickly. If Bigfoot exists, it could be possible they have enough intelligence to gather their dead and bury or conceal it.

Yet another argument is the way Bigfoot just appears and disappears very quickly. Not to go too deeply into really weird stuff like other dimensions, or string theory, in which physicists posit there's at least 10 to 11 other dimensions that coexist with ours. Since we can't see them, it's possible that this creature leaks in and out of our dimension. Read up on all the various texts on quantum theory and your brain will leak out of your ears.

I don't view having an open mind as being gullible. I would much rather be accepting of things and open to the possibility of almost anything, because a closed mind doesn't let in any light. So as far as the Patterson-Gimlin Film is concerned I think that there's a reasonable amount of evidence that it could very well be the real thing. If it were a costume, you'd think somebody would have found it and exposed it by now. Somebody simply confessing that they made the costume means nothing. I can confess to a lot of things too without evidence. I guess it will always be an open question, until Bigfoot walks into the local Walmart.

Charles Pappas

Charles Pappas is the author of It's a Bitter Little World: The Smartest, Toughest, Nastiest Quotes from Film Noir *and* Flying Cars, Zombie Dogs, and Robot Overlords: How World's Fairs and Trade Expos Changed the World.

The Patterson-Gimlin Film is the Zapruder film of cryptozoology. Both were composed by amateurs: The former was shot on a 16mm Kodak Cine 100 camera, and runs 59.5 seconds of the wilderness outside Willow Creek, California, while the latter was captured in color on an 8mm Bell & Howell Zoomatic Director Series Model 414 PD, and captures 26 seconds of the chaos in Dallas. One is of a mythical beast; the other of a fabled president. But both converge in a Venn diagram of fate, because they both achieved pop immortality, and for many of the same reasons.

Grainy and jittery, the films' imperfect — and thus easy to interpret, re-interpret, and re-reinterpret, ad infinitum (it's re-interpretations all the way down!) — visuals keep them alive today to those receptive to conspiracy and those hungry for mystery. For example, in his book *Searching for Sasquatch: Crackpots, Eggheads and Cryptozoology*, Brian Regal, an assistant professor of the history of science at New Jersey's Kean University, nails it: "The low resolution of the original grainy 16mm footage renders it practically impossible to analyze in great detail."

It is both films' forensic-resistant ambiguity that keeps them alive and kicking in the public consciousness 55 years after the JFK assassination and 51 years after the Bigfoot sighting. Max Holland, who wrote *The Kennedy Assassination Tapes*, and Johann Rush, a professional photographer, penned a 2007 *New York Times* editorial arguing the Zapruder film was paused at some point, thereby leaving a gunshot unaccounted for. As recently as 2015, assassination researchers Dale Myers and Todd Vaughn dissed Holland on Myer's blog, shortly after Myers made a public speech on the topic.

Likewise, a quick and dirty search shows the Patterson-Gimlin clip is still being debated from the Huffington Post to Animal Planet to CNET. Its veracity will be discussed and disputed fruitlessly, with the same utter lack of the possibility of resolution as "Did Tony die in *The Sopranos*' finale?"

It's no accident I invoke a popular culture reference here. Popular culture is the fountain of youth both these films drink from with gusto, a beverage keeping them forever fresh. JFK shows up in novels like Dom de Lillo's *Libra* and James Ellroy's *American Tabloid*, movies such as *Forrest Gump* and *X-Men: First Class*, and even as a non-playable character in "Call of Duty: Black Ops." As long as JFK exerts some kind of gravitational pull on the national psyche, the Zapruder film will always be deliberated.

Bigfoot's cultural footprint may be even larger, having stomped across a slew of TV shows and movies: *The Six Million Dollar Man*, *Harry and the Hendersons* (movie and TV show), and *The Simpsons*. There were appearances in the video games "Red Dead Redemption: Undead Nightmare" and "Grand Theft Auto: V." Of more recent vintage was Bigfoot's prominent role in a slew of Jack Link's beef jerky commercials.

The durability of Patterson-Gimlin and Zapruder does not suggest that the American IQ has dropped like the temperature in a Minnesota January. Because conspiracies are plausible; Bigfoot is possible.

The rich and powerful, who have money like beaches have sand, do form hives of scum and villainy at Bohemian Grove, Bilderberg, and Davos to chart the course of the world. Big Tobacco covered up its pleasurable poisons for nearly half a century. The CIA operated Project MKUltra, an actual, for-real mind-control program. Meanwhile, the government recently revealed its clandestine UFO study program, complete with footage that wouldn't seem out of place on *The X-Files*.

The giant squid probably inspired the Scylla of Greek and the kraken of Norse legends. It required 2,000 years from the squid's first sighting until its existence was finally verified in the 1870s. It took until 1910 for the objective reality of the Komodo dragon's existence to be accepted as a textbook-worthy fact by European zoologists. Descriptions of the platypus seemed so farfetched they were dismissed as fake news. Even more notably, coelacanths were thought to have been extinct since the Late Cretaceous era, some 66 million years ago, but were rediscovered off the South Africa coast in 1938.

I said before that Patterson-Gimlin and Zapruder are linked by similar origin stories: both were shot by amateurs. Now, take some of the most famous movies sequences: chariot racing in *Ben Hur*, the shower in *Psycho*, or Danny Torrance pedaling his tricycle in *The Shining*. These were all composed, arranged, and controlled with OCD exactness. But Patterson-Gimlin and Zapruder were happenstance, made by everymen, as much an accident as a hit-and-run. They attest to the idea that we do not have to be auteurs or household names to experience and record the unfathomable and the unforgettable. We only have to stumble into serendipity's path to freeze a moment, and change what we know of reality with the verve of Michelangelo's brush first meeting the Sistine Chapel's blank ceiling.

Felix Vasquez, Jr.

Felix Vasquez, Jr. is the publisher and editor of Cinema Crazed, an online site celebrating all things cinematic.

I fondly remember the first time I ever watched the Patterson-Gimlin footage. I could easily see why it's managed to compel so many generations, since the footage seems so genuine and definitive. It's one of the few pieces of Bigfoot footage that's been tough to contest and it's become iconic for many individuals' inability to disprove it, much in the realm of the Brown Lady of Raynham Hall, the Hopkinsville Goblins, and the Phoenix Lights. There have been so many back and forth discussions on why the footage isn't or is genuine.

Some people have explained that one would have had to have been a bodybuilder to carry such a stature as the alleged Sasquatch that we saw on film, not to mention the people who argue that the Sasquatch is a product of special effects, an amazing creation that was shockingly ahead of its time. It'd be almost like watching Rob Bottin's effects in 1930's cinema. On the one hand, the Bigfoot looks amazing and its walk seems so unique. But on the other hand, there were many stories that one of the men involved in the filming of the footage claimed on his death bed that they'd built a suit for the sake of filming specific footage.

I've seen so many details and studies, including one YouTuber and researcher who claims that if you see the entirety of the footage, not only are there multiple tracks beside the female Sasquatch, but in the distance you can see a smaller ape and another ape of her size hiding in the trees, apparently awaiting her arrival. There are claims by the director that the horses wouldn't go beyond the point they'd reached to film the now iconic reel, so perhaps the horses sensed more than one beast in the trees?

We may never truly know, but the footage is so clear and vivid that, even with its quality and the decades that have passed, it still makes us feel like we're witnessing an awe-inspiring event rife with dangers. Even if the film is one big hoax, the men behind the footage are genius filmmakers, because we learn so much about Bigfoot with one shaky pan of it walking in the wilderness. We learn that it's anthropomorphic, there are the traditional genders of male and female within its species, the women have breasts just like human females. And the mere acknowledgement of the men is what's probably most fascinating. It pays notice to them, but doesn't seem aggressive, but more docile like gorillas or whatnot. Maybe it's social like normal human beings.

Even with all the believers of cryptozoology out there, from the Loch Ness monster to the Mothman, all we have are blurry, often debunked pictures. With the Patterson-Gimlin footage, we have what feels like rock-solid proof. There have been so many accounts of hunters approached by man-like apes. Even Theodore Roosevelt, in 1892, contributed to a book about an encounter by fellow hunters involving a group of ape-like men that terrorized them for nights on end. After fending them off as best as they could for a few nights, the man in the story left for a few hours and returned to his camp to see his hunting partner torn to pieces. It seemed as if he'd been tossed around and murdered pretty viciously. Many theorize it was Roosevelt who was the man in the story, using an alias to avoid being ostracized. We're discovering new species every day on Earth. Who's to say this ape just doesn't exist?

I don't think the footage of the Sasquatch has opened us up to the potential of a colony of ape men are out there. It just sparks the possibility that there's so much left to explore in nature, and this might be the turning point where we learn that our world is bigger than we realize. I don't know if I believe the Patterson-Gimlin footage is concrete proof of the existence of Bigfoot, but I think it's a damn fine example of stellar filmmaking and meticulous scene setting. It's also inspired new generations of explorers, for better or for worse.

Richard Cyr

Richard Cyr is a short-story fiction writer, comic, and host of the podcast The Claw's Corner.

I have always been fascinated with folklore, urban legends, and the unknown. UFOs, aliens, the Loch Ness monster, and Bigfoot are just a few. Growing up, I was most fascinated with Bigfoot. A large part of this is due to the release of the Patterson-Gimlin Film, with its grainy, shaky, and out-of-focus footage of an ape-like creature walking slowly through the woods, then stopping to stare at the camera for a second, before ambling away into the woods.

Many have claimed that Bigfoot is a hoax, but the fact that the same stories regarding sightings are coming from all age groups, socioeconomic backgrounds, and education levels living in many different parts of the world, describing the same creature, is proof to many that Bigfoot is not limited to pranksters.

The film has intrigued people for years, prompting many to come up with their own theories: Bigfoot is an alien or a remnant of the Neanderthal Man. As many believers as Bigfoot has, it also has its share of detractors. A major question that is asked is, "If Bigfoot does actually exist, then why was a skeleton never found, and why has a hunter never run into one?"

I do believe that Bigfoot exists. There are too many people from all over the world reporting the same creature. I don't think that they are all lying. That being said, my belief is that the Patterson-Gimlin Film is a fake. The creature does look like a human in a gorilla suit to me, and there is much evidence to support that opinion.

Whether you are a skeptic or believer of the Patterson-Gimlin Film, there is one word that describes both: fascination. The footage sparked a debate a half-century ago, and it appears that there is no end in sight.

Paul Brenner

Paul Brenner is a film critic whose writing has appeared in The Encyclopedia of Film *and* Magill's Survey of Foreign Language Cinema, *and on FilmCritic.com and Film Racket.com.*

It is a grainy, shaky piece of film footage from October 20, 1967, lasting a minute and a half, 23.85 feet long, coming at the end of the film reel after random footage of horseback riding and scenery. For the first few seconds, the camera is bobbing and hopping as the cameraman rushes through the grass. Then the camera comes to a halt and the image balances, revealing a seemingly tall, hairy human/ape creature striding on the other side of a stream. At one point (Frame 352) the creature pauses to glance into the camera. Then it moves on past the stream and into the brush. Here the film reel ends.

The chilling aspect of the footage is that the creature saunters through the frame not so much as a hairy, apelike being (with breasts), but strolls with ease, like Bob Hope or Jack Benny striding out on stage to deliver a comedy routine. Then comes the look into the camera, as if a television director in a booth told the thing to look in Camera 3 and get ready for a closeup.

Is this footage a gag? Gag or not, the legendary Roger Patterson-Bob Gimlin footage is (along with the Zapruder film which captured the assassination of John F. Kennedy) is the last of a breed — allegedly documentary proof of an atypical event, before Photoshop and CGI and Russian bots rendered any truth just a set of alternative facts. And like the Zapruder film (which may or may not have provided evidence of a second gunman), the Patterson-Gimlin Film is also truth in the eye of the beholder. Is that apelike creature the legendary Bigfoot, or is it a tall guy in a monkey suit stolen from the wardrobe department of *2001: A Space Odyssey* or *Planet of the Apes*?

The Patterson-Gimlin Film's last mystery is perhaps the Bigfoot glance at Frame 352. The footage gives hope that there is still some mystery left in a world of new cycles and spin, just the thing for an era of fake news. While talk of a deep state and FBI cabals sends fear up and down the spines of people looking at the daily news feed, Bigfoot is as comforting as Grandma's meatloaf. And it is not just you. Matt LeBlanc is a believer, and House Majority Leader Kevin McCarthy happily poses with a guy in a Bigfoot suit.

Frame 352 connects with the Dawn of Man and sanctifies a humanoid fake-out, ecstatically joining hands with the scope of world literature. A Bigfoot-like creature appears in Gilgamesh and the Bible (Esau is described as "red all over like a hairy garment"). Medieval literature featured fairies and Green Men, and Rousseau writes of "a noble savage." Bigfoot-like creatures appear in Virgil, Horace, Petrach and Boccacio, Spencer, and Marlowe. And who is Caliban in Shakespeare's *The Tempest* but a Bigfoot that speaks the King's English in highfalutin' tones? Bigfoot is universal, crossing all cultures, hiding in the deep shadows of the human psyche. The Patterson-Gimlin Film acts a restorative, emerging as a powerful force of popular culture in the bleak times of the Vietnam War, Watergate, Irangate, 9/11, and on into the polarized political system of today.

The Patterson-Gimlin Film, ultimately disproved, still carries on and, as John Ford knows, "When the legend becomes fact, print the legend." Raymond Williams has written that for popular legends, "myth functions as memory." And myth has washed over the Patterson-Gimlin Film and made it clean, much as the Zapruder film will for believers forever reveal a second gunman's bullet trajectory.

Bigfoot products have been amassed through the years, perhaps surpassing the warehouse holding the detritus of Charles Foster Kane's life in *Citizen Kane* or the storage facility holding the Ark of the Covenant in *Raiders of the Lost Ark*. Besides the usual books and t-shirts, a brief tour of Amazon reveals such consumer flotsam and jetsam as Bigfoot Trackers ("use in snow, sand and mud"), hot sauce, cookie cutters, air fresheners, Bigfoot research kits, stuffed Bigfoots, lounge pajamas, socks, Don't Feed the Bigfoot signs, electronic noisemakers, orthopedic canes, action figures, costume feet, scooters, playing cards, Christmas ornaments, beanies, wrapping paper, playlets, lunch boxes, bobbleheads, toy cars, hats, Lego sets, magnets, ice cream makers, bandages, soap, Dr. Dentons, scarfs, notebooks, tiki mugs, GI Joe figures, mints, freebies and magnets. Apparently, the only products not yet Bigfoot-oriented are condoms and defibrillators.

British physicist Michael Faraday has written, "To seek such evidence and appearances as are in the favor of our desires, and to disregard those which oppose them ... We reserve as friendly that which argues with us, we resist and dislike that which opposes us; whereas the very reverse is required by every dictate of common sense." In the age of instant and questionable information, Bigfoot is reassuring to people who feel that uncritical thinking is comforting.

The rivers of facts are muddied and it is hard to see anything for what is it anymore. If we could all only be like Kirk Douglas in the 1954 film *Ulysses*. Douglas, playing Ulysses, is walking with his warriors on a deserted beach when one of his men comes across the footprint of the giant Cyclops. He asks, "Ulysses, who could have made such a big footprint?" Douglas replies, without a trace of irony, "A man with big feet?"

A Bigfoot Interlude: Chanel for Sasquatch?

In September 2017, Marion, North Carolina-based wife and mother Allie Megan Webb turned entrepreneur by introducing Bigfoot Juice to the market. Pricing the product at $7.00 a bottle, Webb claimed that the potion could attract a Sasquatch by appealing to its olfactory senses.

"How do you know it works?" Webb said. "That's a tough question. I guess I could ask how do you know it doesn't work?"

Webb insisted that the product was tested by Bigfoot 911, a research group on the hunt for you-know-what in the woods of North Carolina's McDowell County. The group sprayed some Bigfoot Juice on themselves – the potion doubles as insect repellent – and claimed that the scent helped them spot a Sasquatch in the forest.

"I think that's enough to say it can attract a Bigfoot," says Webb. "To attract a Bigfoot, you need a smell that is woodsy enough to keep from scaring him off. But slightly different enough to make him curious, and come to investigate."

Chapter Seven
The Show is Over

"Exit, stage left." – Snagglepuss

As of this writing, Bob Gimlin makes occasional appearances at conferences devoted to the celebration of all things Bigfoot. Not surprisingly, he is treated like a rock star by the attendees at these events.

René Dahinden died in April 2001 from prostate cancer. In a newspaper obituary, he was recalled by a friend who said Dahinden looked back on his life's pursuit of Bigfoot and muttered, "You know, I've spent over 40 years — and I didn't find it. I guess that's got to say something."

In the years following the release of the Bigfoot footage, Al DeAtley has mostly avoided making any public comment on his involvement with brother-in-law Roger Patterson, and his very few interviews suggested that he had some degree of remorse in bringing the Patterson-Gimlin Film to the world. In a February 1999 interview with the *Yakima Herald-Record*, he was asked if he believed the Bluff Creek footage was genuine. "I never asked," he said, "because I didn't want to know." DeAtley's last published interview on the subject was in Greg Long's 2004 book *The Making of Bigfoot*, in which he stated, "I never wanted to know if it was a hoax. I don't want to know, and I never got myself into a position to know or not to know. I didn't want to be part of something that I assumed was happening."

Bob Heironimus, who claimed to be Bigfoot in the Patterson-Gimlin Film, and Philip Morris, who claimed to have sold Roger Patterson a costume that was used in the 1967 film, appeared on a November 2016 Internet radio broadcast called "Hoax of the Century" to repeat their insistence that the Bluff Creek footage was staged. The broadcast was coordinated by Tom Biscardi, who produced the film 2012 documentary *Hoax of the Century* and who hosted the broadcast, which also included Bigfoot-focused writers Greg Long and Michael Greene. "This landmark radio program will irrefutably prove that the Patterson-Gimlin film was perpetrated upon the public as a hoax for monetary benefit," stated Biscardi in a press release announcing the broadcast.

Bigfoot: America's Abominable Snowman, Roger Patterson's 1969 feature-length film that included the BBC documentary which incorporated the Patterson-Gimlin Film, was never released in any home entertainment format. Although the BBC no longer maintains a copy of its original documentary – many British television programs of that era were not preserved and are considered lost – the network still maintains the copyright to its footage. The International Cryptozoology Museum in Portland, Maine, has a print in its collection and is willing to offer private screenings for researchers.

The Sasquatch of Bluff Creek was never seen again after turning its back on Patterson and Gimlin and wandering away into the woods. Whatever became of it is anyone's guess. Did it rejoin a band of fellow Sasquatches in an endless odyssey through the California woods, evading detection from those strange bipeds desperate to make contact? Or did it slip into a solitary existence, cut off from its species – and, perhaps, as the last of its species, live out its days in a tragic pursuit of companionship that could never be fulfilled?

Or did the Sasquatch loosen buttons and zippers around its neck and torso, peeling away its temporary identity to become a man once again? Did the human occupant of the furry suit wipe away the sweat from the costume enclosure, resume his proper clothing, and shove the temporary animal covering back into its storage box amid smirks and giggles at the genius trick being played?

In the half-century since the Patterson-Gimlin Film was shot, opinion remains stubbornly divided between those who embrace the reality of the Sasquatch with unwavering gusto and those who shake their heads in astonishment at the perceived gullibility of the other side.

Which side is right? If you've made it this far into this book, you might have noticed that neither side has been happily advocated or brutally condemned. This is not because the author is absent of an opinion, but because the question of whether or not the film is a fraud is not the right question to ask.

Instead, a better query would be: What are we really looking at when we watch the Patterson-Gimlin Film? Would it be flippant to suggest that it should not be viewed as a ribbon of celluloid, but instead as a mirror where one's intellectual and emotional state is reflected back?

Film viewing is the ultimate act of subjective consideration. The filmmakers labor to present a vision, but that does not mean the viewer shares their vision. No one is to blame here on the disconnect. It is equally possible that the creative artist has a misguided sense of contextual importance, or the viewers are too prejudiced not to color their visions with their own ideas of what's right and what's not.

When looking at the Patterson-Gimlin Film, are we looking at an insouciant Sasquatch meandering away from the first and only motion picture camera to document its existence? If that's the case, then we believe that we're witnesses to a miracle: Patterson and Gimlin stumbled into the wildest detour in the history of zoology, offering us irrefutable proof that man's knowledge of his fellow species is riddled with holes large enough for a Sasquatch to walk through. The film would also require a new consideration of whether legends and reality exist with blurred boundaries rather than thickly defined borders. After all, the Sasquatch on the screen would affirm that the most extreme flights of folkloric imagination were not the product of alleged primitive peoples having too much fun with their religious fantasies.

But what if the Patterson-Gimlin Film is a fake? What does that say about the two men who emerged from Bluff Creek to tell the world about the remarkable thing they saw and filmed? Did Patterson go to his early death as a chronic liar, holding on tightly to a brilliant hoax until his life was brought to a cancerous conclusion? And is Gimlin still living a ridiculous lie, giving interviews and making appearances at Bigfoot-focused expos without betraying a modicum of remorse for being a fraud? And if this is the case, what would all of this say about the people who have accepted the idea that Bigfoot is somewhere out there – were these people idiots for believing such a tale?

On the surface, the Patterson-Gimlin Film forces the viewer to confront a bizarre sight and demand an opinion that falls into one of two very different choices. There is no right or wrong answer, as both choices come with heavy burdens that cannot be easily alleviated. Accept the Sasquatch on the screen as real and your detractors will label you as a fool who will believe any fairy tale as long as it runs through a film projector. Reject the Sasquatch and you run the risk of being called a cynic whose slavish devotion to chiseled-in-stone science was disproven by a pair of ex-rodeo riders with a borrowed camera and a surplus of good luck.

Perhaps both the problem and the beauty of the film is the fact that it was not the work of scientists in the midst of a well-orchestrated expedition, but of a pair of amateurs who bumbled their way into a one-in-a-million situation. The film's longtime supporters insist that it was impossible for Patterson and Gimlin to create and maintain a charade of such elaborate dimensions. Likewise, the film's equally devoted detractors insist that the being on screen is too obviously a man in an ape suit, adding that Patterson and Gimlin only succeeded in confirming that classic H.L. Mencken observation, "No one ever went broke underestimating the intelligence of the American people."

Ultimately, this debate becomes a carousel conversation that spins around and around endlessly, leaving its participants back where they began rather than taking them to a new plateau of insight and enlightenment. It's a lose-lose situation if one persists in traveling this rocky path.

Maybe the viewer should follow the lead of the Bluff Creek Sasquatch and just walk away from the whole thing, heading off to another horizon without looking back or giving a second thought to the troubles created by the camera following its journey?

Yeah, if only things were that easy!

Acknowledgements

This book is being presented to you through the good graces of BearManor Media and its publisher, Ben Ohmart. I am grateful that Ben was willing to tiptoe outside of his comfort zone in releasing this admittedly off-beat book. And I am grateful for Robbie Adkins of Adkins Consulting for doing such an amazing job in making my book look good.

The Bigfoot illustrations within this book are by José Daniel Oviedo Galeano, a talented artist based in Colombia. It was a pleasure working with him on this project.

I am also grateful for Mary Brown's input in the copyediting process, and for Clint Weiler's work in helping to promote this work and my earlier BearManor Media books.

Rob Firsching provided invaluable insight for the chapter on Bigfoot-inspired cinema, and his contribution is greatly appreciated. I also need to give a hat-tip to Loren Coleman for information on Roger Patterson's elusive feature-length documentary that incorporated BBC footage into the mix.

My friends and family have been a rock of support throughout my adventures in the media world, and no words could adequately express the gratitude I have for their love and encouragement.

And, in the event that Bigfoot is still out there somewhere in the Bluff Creek area, here's a shout-out of good cheer, and the hope that this beloved hominid manages to stay one very big step ahead of the human race!

Bibliography

"Bigfoot and a Missionary." *Sasquatch and Bigfoot: Facts and History*, January 9, 2014.

Blu Buhs, Joshua. "Bigfoot: The Life and Times of a Legend." *University of Chicago Press*, 2009.

Cantrall, Thom. "21 Days to Destiny: The Real Story of Bluff Creek." *RS Publishing*, 2015.

Chorvinsky, Mark. "The Makeup Man and the Monster: John Chambers and the Patterson Bigfoot Suit." *Strange Magazine*, Summer 1996.

Chorvinsky, Mark. "UPDATE: Film Director John Landis Goes Public Concerning Makeup Master John Chambers' Involvement In The Famous Patterson Bigfoot Film." *Strange Report #6*, October 6, 1997.

Coleman, Loren. "Bigfoot Researcher Bobbie Short Has Died." *Cryptozoo News*, March 23, 3013.

De Moraes, Lisa. "TV critics suspicious about Animal Planet's 'Finding Bigfoot.'" *Washington Post*, August 2, 2012.

Driscoll, John. "The Birth of Bigfoot." *The Times-Standard*, October 30, 2008.

Ebert, Roger. "Big Foot." *Chicago Sun-Times*, January 1971.

"Ep. 25: Kidnapped by Bigfoot: The Albert Ostman Story." *Astonishing Legends*, October 9, 2015.

Firsching, Robert. "Bigfoot Cinema." Unpublished essay.

Hall, Phil. "The Bootleg Files: The 1950 Montana UFO Film." *Film Threat*, January 11, 2013.

Hall, Phil. "The Bootleg Files: The Patterson-Gimlin Film." *Film Threat*, November 8, 2007.

Hill, Kyle. "Why Bigfoot is Unlikely Only If You Know What 'Unlikely' Means." *Scientific American*, October 1, 2013.

"The Holy Bible: New International Version." *Zondervan Publishing House*, 1984.

"Idaho woman says Bigfoot sighting caused her to crash into deer." *Associated Press/New York Daily News*, March 25, 2017.

Levs, Josh. "Bigfoot hoax ends in death, authorities say." *CNN*, August 28, 2012.

Long, Greg. "The Making of Bigfoot." *Prometheus Books*, 2004.

Martin, David, and Boyd, Alistair. "Nessie – The Surgeon's Photograph Exposed." *Books for Dillons Only*, 1999.

Maslin, Janet. "Film: 'Sasquatch' Roams Northwest:Monster Search." *New York Times*, January 12, 1978.

Meyers, Donald W. "It Happened Here: The legend of Sasquatch has footprints in Yakima." *Yakima Herald*, October 29, 2017.

Moye, David. "Jane Goodall 'Fascinated' By Bigfoot." *Huffington Post*, October 1, 2012.

"Mrs. Bigfoot is Filmed!" *The Times-Standard*, October 21, 1967.

Munns, William. "When Roger Met Patty." *CreateSpace*, 2014.

Murphy, Christopher L. "Bigfoot Journal." *Hancock House*, 2008.

Patterson, Roger. "Do Abominable Snowmen in America Really Exist?" *Pyramid Publications*, 1996 (reissue).

Price, Mark. "NC mom invents a spray she says will attract any Bigfoot within a mile and a half." *Charlotte Observer*, September 13, 2017.

Price, Mark. "Shaman clad in animal skins claims he was mistaken for NC Bigfoot. Some doubt it." *Charlotte Observer*, August 10, 2017.

Roosevelt, Theodore. "The Wilderness Hunter." Leopold Classic Library, 2016 (reissue).

Rosman, John. "Film Introducing Bigfoot To World Still Mysterious 50 Years Later." *OPB*, December 20, 2017.

Sanderson, Ivan T. "First Photos of Bigfoot, California's Legendary 'Abominable Snowman.'" *Argosy*, February 1968.

"Sasquatch Classics: The William Roe Encounter." *Sasquatch Chronicles Blog*, January 2015.

"Search for Sasquatch lands two men in trouble." *Lebanon Daily News*, May 10, 2012.

Shackley, Myra. "Still Living? Yeti, Sasquatch and the Neanderthal Enigma." *W.W. Norton & Co.*, 1986.

Sotille, Leah. "The Man Who Created Bigfoot." *Outside*, July 5, 2016.

Strauss, Mark. "The Largest Ape That Ever Lived Was Doomed By Its Size." *National Geographic*, January 5, 2016.

"Talk of the Nation: Science Friday – Dr. Jane Goodall." *National Public Radio*, September 27, 2002.

"The Ape Canyon Incident of 1924." *Sasquatch Chronicles Blog*, April 17, 2015.

"The oldest account of Bigfoot was recorded in 986 AD." *Sasquatch Chronicles Blog*, August 28, 2015.

"The Search Goes on for Bigfoot." *Smithsonian*, January 1974.

Truet, Turin, and Gilman, Laura Anne. "Searching for Yeti: The Abominable Snowman." *Rosen Central*, 2001.

Wayman, Erin. "Did Bigfoot Really Exist? How Gigantopithecus Became Extinct." *Smithsonian*, January 9, 2012.

About the Author

Phil Hall is the author of seven books, including the BearManor Media releases *The History of Independent Cinema*, *What If They Lived?* (co-written with Rory L. Aronsky), *The Greatest Bad Movies of All Time*, and *In Search of Lost Films*. His cinema writing has been published in *The New York Times*, *New York Daily News*, *Wired*, and *American Movie Classics Magazine*, and his weekly film history column "The Bootleg Files" appears every Friday on the Cinema Crazed website.

Phil Hall is also the host and producer of *The Online Movie Show with Phil Hall*, which can be heard on SoundCloud, and he formerly served on the Governing Committee of the Online Film Critics Society.